"The Baby Boomerang offers a road map to the hearts and souls of a missing generation."
George Barna

The Baby Boomerang

Doug Murren

Catching Baby Boomers as They Return to Church

Regal Books
A Division of Gospel Light
Ventura, California, U.S.A.

Published by Regal Books
A Division of GL Publications
Ventura, California 93006

Library of Congress Cataloging-in-Publication Data

Murren, Doug, 1951-
  The baby boomerang : catching the baby boomers as they return to church / by Doug Murren.
      p.   cm.
  Includes bibliographical references.
  ISBN 0-8307-1395-6
  1. Baby boom generation—Religious life.   I. Title.
BV4529.2.M87   1990
250'.973'09049—dc20   90-46029
                                                                          CIP

4 5 6 7 8 9 10 / X3 / KP / 95 94 93 92 91

Rights for publishing this book in other languages are contracted by Gospel Literature International (GLINT) foundation. GLINT also provides technical help for the adaptation, translation, and publishing of Bible study resources and books in scores of languages worldwide. For further information, contact GLINT, Post Office Box 488, Rosemead, California, 91770, U.S.A., or the publisher.

CONTENTS

PREFACE

"Whether these are the worst of times or the best of times, they are the only times we have."
—Art Buchwald

THE '80s have been described by some observers as a rehash of the '60s and '70s. And one prominent critic labeled the era "The 'Me' Decade." But I'll toss my hat in the ring with those who characterize the late '80s and early '90s as the ascendancy of the '60s culture, as the coming of age of the spirit of 1968.

BOOMER CULTURE

Charles Kaiser in his book, *1968 in America*, declared: "What happened in 1968 was the most turbulent 12 months in the postwar period and one of the most disturbing intervals we have lived through since the Civil War."[1]

Dr. R. C. Sproul quotes Os Guiness, one of the noted L'Abri scholars of that era, as saying that this cultural shift, which began in the '60s and continues with unabated force today, equals the Civil War in its revolutionary impact on American culture.

The New Age movement, the rise of the self-potential culture, the wildly Eastern tone in our sciences and the new make-your-own religions are all signs of the rise and legitimization of the '60s worldview. *Newsweek* magazine ran a cover story on September 5, 1988 entitled, "Will We Ever Get over the '60s?" It dealt with the shock and impact of this generation, whose members are known variously as yuppies, grumpies and dinks, but usually as boomers.

BOOMER POWER

But why all this attention to boomers? Because they represent more than just an age issue. They comprise a whole new cultural paradigm that, in turn, spells "boomer power."

And boomer power isn't just coming; it has come. It is here.

That's why tunes and records from the '60s are being re-released on CDs with astonishing success. And that's also why any book or magazine that runs the words "baby boomer" is promised at least a better-than-average year. Their sales are also signs that a large portion of our culture group is trying to come to grips with its own maturation.

Boomer power is why nearly everyone from marketing firms and political parties to educational institutions is seeking to understand the power and peculiarities of this culture group, of this now nearly middle-aged generation. You see, at least 78 million people in America have been shaped by the culture identified with the 1960s. And they will be the power brokers of American society well into the next century. If for no other reason than for their sheer numbers, they dwarf both the generations that preceded them and that of their own children.

BOOMER AWARENESS

Even though I'm a baby boomer myself, I hate the name. There really aren't enough yuppies to even talk about them. And maybe there are some grumpies and dinks, but basically we are all baby boomers. We are just folks with a worldview that was shaped by the history our generation came through.

As I said, I am a boomer myself. And, though I am not a sociologist or otherwise academically qualified to predict trends, I am also a pastor to boomers, for our church has had to aim itself at this group. Why have we at Eastside Church done so?

First, in the early 1980s, our church began attracting people in their mid-30s and younger. At that time, it hadn't even occurred to me that baby boomers and thirty something people were one and the same. I had done some reading about boomers, but I had never given much thought to them as a group. In time, however, I discovered that these baby boomers are tremendously open to Christ and to the life of the Church when they understand our message.

BOOMER OUTREACH

Second, in realizing that baby boomers are nearly one-third of the total United States population, we recognized that reaching this vast number for Christ represented an unparalleled opportunity given to the Church in this decade of the twentieth century for an evangelism outreach to the unchurched.

Third, a few years ago I was asked to give a lecture on how our church was reaching out to baby boomers. As I prepared for that lecture, I became more impassioned about the various available opportunities for reaching people my age. And after I gave the lecture, I received invitations from all over the country to speak on "Baby Boomers in the Church."

Along the way, I met numbers of others who were also articulating ways to reach boomers and received words of encouragement from people all over America as well. The favorable response to a couple of articles in my *Ministries Today* column about steps churches can take to reach boomers brought another wave of encouragement.

I gave a series of talks on this topic of baby boomers and the Church. A Presbyterian church in the Los Angeles area taped my talks, made 250 copies of the tapes and gave them out to their membership in preparation for a five-year plan.

Some of those tapes passed into the hands of another older congregation that was rapidly dwindling away. After listening to my tapes, that congregation voted to turn their church over to a younger pastor who would give new direction to its ministry, aiming it at baby boomers. In a short time attendance at that church swelled to over 400 persons.

I was so excited and gratified after hearing this story that it motivated me to take the content of those talks and put it into a book that would guide churches and baby boomers on how to get together. That book is the one you now hold.

I have written with the intent of providing an understanding of key features of the boomer's belief system that will enable the Church to respond appropriately. I have also written with the hope of helping people of my generation understand why the Church seems so foreign and so difficult for them to participate in, yet with the expectation that they will continue to seek and to find those churches which match their expectations and anticipations of church life.

Today, much of the church world is trying to come to grips with the phenomenon of the boomer revolution, even as boomers are trying to make sense of the Church. Maybe hearing from a boomer pastor will help some to do so. I pray it will.

Note

1. Charles Kaiser, "Introduction," *1968 in America: Music Politics, Chaos, Counterculture and the Shaping of a Generation* (New York, NY: Weidenfeld & Nicolson, 1988), p. xv.

An Introduction Meant to Be Read

"As it washes up into the 1980s, the baby boom generation has experienced a shift in the way it thinks about itself and its future."

—Tom Hayden[1]

I entered the all-night restaurant, sat down in a booth and slid over the hard vinyl seat. It felt greasy and unclean. Noting the grime, then forgetting it quickly, I greeted my guest, who was already seated. He was a pastor of long-standing in the Kirkland, Washington community.

I'd asked to meet with him because I was contemplating pioneering a church in Kirkland. I was at least 20 years his junior. I was also broke, without a plan and somewhat disillusioned from an all-too-recent bad church-staff experience. Yet, somehow, I was determined to try again.

I had been certain the older pastor would embrace a new "soldier of the Lord" in town with great joy. I was quite surprised and certainly unprepared when I realized that he regarded me more as a potential rival than as a prospective colleague. That I would ever be viewed as a threat or as competition by another pastor had never occurred to me.

UNDERSTANDING OUR COMMUNITY

Now, several years later, I can understand his sentiment. The intensity of the pastoral call does make one cautious about any newcomer in town expressing the desire to shepherd a flock. To think of laying aside such a commitment is difficult when confronted by a younger, naive-looking pastor who might put a crimp in your own plans. I understand all that now, though I didn't then.

So I began the conversation, "Hi, pastor. I would like to get some input from you before I formulate plans for pioneering a church in town. We've just begun a study which seems to be working quite well, and I'd like to ask you a few questions."

He responded, "I don't think this town needs another witness of this sort." I wasn't sure what he meant by "witness of this sort."

"What is your plan? Where do you plan to locate? What kind of people are you going to target?" he queried.

His last question caught my attention. I'd never thought about a "target" group of people. Yet not wanting to appear as dumb as I felt, I simply responded: "Well, I think I'd like to reach people like myself—those who have some difficulty relating to the traditional church setting. You know, younger people."

His eyes flashed, revealing immediately that he didn't like hearing my remark. After all, was I implying that he was too old to reach people in my age group? With obviously controlled kindness in his voice, which his eyes belied, he commented, "Well, this is a great area for it."

At that time, in 1979, studies showed that nearly 95 percent of the people in our Bellevue/Kirkland area did not attend any kind of church. So even that tiny spark of encouragement tossed to me by that pastor meant a lot to me. However, had I depended entirely on this conversation as the basis for continuing, I wouldn't have.

Yet, over the years I have looked back on that conversation with a great deal of fondness. Why? Because it forced me to answer these important questions:

- Who were we going to reach? and
- Why were we in this city?

Three months later, this same scene was nearly duplicated, but this time on more friendly terms. I drove down to Portland, Oregon, about three hours south of Seattle, to meet a highly successful pastor in our Foursquare denomination. We sat down together at a nice restaurant and both ordered taco salad.

Getting acquainted, we exchanged small talk at first. Then all at once he asked, "Well, what can I do for you? We've got an hour. Let's make the most of it."

> *These are the very first questions any pioneer pastor or, for that matter, any leader of any church should ask: Is this church supposed to be here? If so, what unique expression will it bring to this community?*

The abruptness of his question startled me. I was hoping he would clarify some of my concerns, but I wasn't prepared for such directness as I was still trying to decide how to establish a congregation. And initially, I wasn't so sure I even wanted to pastor anymore, though our home Bible study was going quite well, numbering some 30 people.

I stammered as I answered, "Well, we're just beginning to formulate our plans."

Smiling to ease the tension I was feeling, he countered, "Well, what are you supposed to be in that community that isn't already there? After all, God is never redundant."

I'm greatly indebted to that pastor—now not only my friend, but also a member of our staff—for helping me address that question of purpose. That phrase, "God is never redundant" haunted me for weeks, as I pondered the need for an Eastside Church.

FORMULATING OUR PLAN AND PURPOSE

At the time I thought it was uncanny that the topics of plan and purpose had come up again. But I now realize these are the very first questions any pioneer pastor or, for that matter, any leader of any church should ask:

- Is this church supposed to be here?
- If so, what unique expression will it bring to this community?

As I jotted the questions down with a green pen on a yellow pad, I felt more and more ill-prepared to reach out effectively in our area. Nevertheless, as our conversation continued, I pondered and posed questions on how I could discern what my mission ought to be in our community.

I came away with this list:

- What are the needs to be met in this community that presently aren't being addressed?
- What age group is particularly open to the ministry style and approach I would be offering?
- What sort of new church would address these needs in our community?

BEGINNING OUR ADVENTURE

Three to four weeks later I called together our ministry team—the leaders of our church-planting adventure. The five of us sat around our coffee table, drinking mocha coffee and munching peanut butter cookies. As we slurped and gulped our goodies, I shared an outline of how I felt we should proceed.

As we progressed through our agenda, we realized the necessity of establishing a clear focus as to why we were here. I suggested that we "key in" on people 35 and younger. At the time of this discussion, we didn't even know we were baby boomers or to describe ourselves as "thirty somethings." After all, this was 10 years before such language was in vogue.

My good friend, Gordon, responding to my suggestion, spoke up. "I think that's a great idea! For one thing, I hope our church is a lot different from what I've experienced."

Tom, who later left to pioneer his own church in California, added, "I hope we can be as evangelistic as possible."

The thought never occurred to us at that time to collect demographic information, a process that is now a vital part of our continuing evaluation of ourselves. Intuitively, we discussed what we felt was needed in our community. We'd each visited several churches in the area and had noted very, very few people our age in any of them. For the most part, the Church was made up of people 10 to 20 years our senior, with only a smattering of uninvolved and unassimilated people our age in attendance.

In fact, most of the people I'd grown up with had never gone to church. Or, if they had, it was for only a short time. I remember one friend in high school who did go—occasionally. Every time he got into trouble and had to go to confession, he got a new pair of shoes and new jeans—sometimes even a haircut. A standing joke among us was that, if Lawrence got new pants and shoes, religion was next!

Yet, we knew there was a lot of life in many churches and that many people were meeting the Lord; for, in the same community, we continually ran into people who were born again, but who had not committed themselves to any fellowship.

ESTABLISHING OUR IDENTITY

We all concluded we needed a church that we ourselves would want to attend. But what kind of church would that be?

I looked across the room to my wife, Debbie, and said, "Well, let's make a list of what makes up the kind of church we would want to go to." She began writing.

Of course, we thought we were primarily discussing biblical emphases. But I'm convinced now that we were outlining cultural preferences as much as anything—nothing unbiblical, but the items discussed were as much cultural as biblical. Our list grew, and we ended up with concerns that essentially match the key points I've outlined in this book on how to reach the baby boomer generation.

- Deb: "We'd like a church with great music."
- Gordon: "We need a great P.A. system. I like good sound. I think people our age do."
- Tom: "We need a place that really has a lot of love and that is an accepting and forgiving place."
- Patty: "We need a church that really cares about kids and hurting people."
- Doug: "We need a church that models serving leadership. We won't be bossing people around and running their lives for them, but we will provide models and instruction to help shape a Christ-centered life philosophy."

We knew now we wouldn't be redundant, for now we had a mission. We had a clear target. We had already accomplished a couple of vital tasks and didn't even know it. Our plan and our philosophy were clear. Now it was up to the Holy Spirit, working through us, to extend His touch to people who were in need and who were hungry for Him.

UTILIZING OUR QUALITIES

I had no idea when we began our church that we were utilizing the qualities that would attract a given generation called "baby boomers." Yet, because we did so, the ensuing eight years became a wonderful adventure. After the first year, exciting things began to happen. Within a one-month period, we added as many as 300 new people to our new church! We have continued to grow rapidly within those eight years to a congregation now numbering 3,500 people.

We've experienced a merger with two similar pioneer churches, with my pastoring the combined flocks. We've also had several entire churches join our own burgeoning flock along the way, bringing with them their pastors and church leadership.

For several years, we remained very narrow in our growth pattern. Then we discovered a very interesting phenomenon, something common to most human dimensions: After we'd grown to a certain size we decided to spread and broaden our appeal and approach, becoming quite effective at reaching the thirty something folks.

MARKETING OUR CHURCH

The baby boomer generation is just now coming to terms with itself. The leadership of major political parties in our country started several years ago to wrestle with the voting power of this boomer generation. For example, Lee Atwater's guitar exhibitions during George Bush's inaugural night celebrations were an ingenious move to catch the ear of this generation. Feeble gesture though it was, it was at least an attempt by the current administration.

The Church, however, has yet to design methods that will deliberately include and involve this baby boomer culture—so immense that it will shape the culture of the Unit-

---

More than at any other time, it is now possible for churches to reach out and minister successfully to the baby boomer generation—if the churches are ready and willing to rise to what is both a great need and a challenging opportunity.

---

ed States from this point on. That the Church has still not done so only emphasizes that the Church has yet to grasp satisfactorily the impact of this boomer generation.

I can't really say that, through a profound and intelligent marketing strategy, I decided to target this age-group deliberately. I simply concluded, after a lot of heart-searching, that the Lord had called us to reach this age-group in their early 40s and younger. At that time, of course, we were 33 and younger ourselves. Our music style, the decor of our building, everything about our church focused toward an age-group that our church very much needed—one that I personally felt the most comfortable about reaching.

Admittedly, the thought of targeting a group of people troubles some. In fact, marketing language troubled me a great deal in the beginning. The first time I explained to our church council that I really felt we had been targeting people, ages 26 to 44 in our community, everyone looked at me with surprised expressions that said, "What's the matter? Don't you like older people or children?"

I find I consciously have to reiterate to our church leaders the conversation we had around that coffee table in 1979. I can think of one leadership council meeting in particular when we rented a conference room of sorts in a nice restaurant for the occasion. I began by stating that I felt we ought to return to and reaffirm the premise and assumptions upon which we began our congregation. I really felt the Lord wanted us to continue to be clear about whom we were focusing our ministry toward in our community. We had deliberately aimed at those who, by and large, have trouble relating to the traditional Church—the thirty something crowd whom the Lord had called us to reach out to specifically.

Sharon, one of our leaders sitting across the room from me, asked, "Well, does this mean I'm ruled out. After all, I'm 46 now."

John Smith, a TV personality in our area who was definitely beyond our years, interjected, "I'm not giving up quite that easily."

Though we all had a great laugh, I knew further explanation was needed, so I hastened to add: "I don't think we're talking about chronological age. I think we're talking about a culture, a mentality that was considered 'illegitimate' in the '60s, that had become 'legitimized' in the '80s. It's the boomer worldview we're talking about. Several of you wouldn't be in this church if you weren't comfortable with that kind of worldview."

When everyone present accepted my explanation. I breathed a sigh of relief, thinking to myself, *Whew! I'm glad I got through that one!*

REACHING OUR GENERATION

We all really knew we weren't talking strictly about an actual age span. We were talking about a cultural phenomenon, a set of attitudes and assumptions, a mentality distinctive to those born between 1946 and 1964. We are the generation of the Vietnam War; of the Kent State University tragedy; of the flower people and drugs; of the assassinations of President John F. Kennedy, Senator Robert F. Kennedy and Rev. Martin Luther King, Jr.; and of the Watergate scandal that forced President Richard Nixon to abdicate in shame—events that shaped our cultural experiences and preferences.

Unlike our parents, we were able to aspire beyond sheer survival. Unlike our grandparents who survived the Great Depression with its worries of having enough food to eat and keeping a roof over their heads, we were able to look ahead and discuss such things as values and dreams. The struggles of our own parents to have a refrigerator, a full freezer and a second car in the garage seemed like boring pursuits to us. We scoffed at owning material things and at pursuing jobs and careers.

We are possibly the most spoiled generation ever to come along. At times our great optimism is challenged by the practical rigors of life. But underlying everything else is still a great upsurge of spirit in the boomer generation which heard Martin Luther King, Jr. cry out: "I have a dream."

In the 1990s, the culture of the boomer generation will not only become legitimized; it will also be empowered and unleashed. We baby boomers of the culture of *Rolling Stone* magazine, of the Hula-Hoop, of John F. Kennedy and of that dream for African-Americans are just now beginning to flex our muscles and test our strength. That is why most demographers agree that the culture of the boomer generation is just now beginning to dominate U.S. culture and will continue to do so well into the next century.

Churches that don't take this baby boomer phenomenon into account will look even more antiquated and irrelevant in years to come. The need to address this generation is a given for marketers, a dilemma for sociologists and society, and a quandary for economists. But only now is the Church commencing to address the all-important and potentially controversial question: How do we, as the Body of Christ, relate to the baby boomer generation?

Being both a churchman and a boomer born right in the middle of the boom, I find myself presently very concerned for my generation. True, this generation left the Church in unprecedented numbers. But now it is likewise returning to the Church in surprising numbers.

So, more than at any other time, it is now possible for churches to reach out and minister successfully to the baby boomer generation—if the churches are ready and willing to rise to what is both a great need and a challenging opportunity. For some churches and denominations, major retooling—reorganization—may first be necessary.

Again, more than at any other time, it is now possible for churches to reach out and minister effectively to us baby boomers. The only requirements are: a willing heart and some essential understanding of our outlook. Major retooling will occur during this decade to embrace us. So let's move ahead and, with the aid of some practical suggestions, commence our reorganization together.

But first, in this next chapter, let's take time to discover and examine why my baby boomer generation is so unique.

Note
1. Tom Hayden, "Decade Shock," *Newsweek*, September 5, 1988, p. 14.

WHAT'S SO SPECIAL ABOUT A BABY BOOMER?

"We are the people of this generation raised in at least modest comfort, housed now in universities, looking uncomfortably to the world we inherit."

—Tom Hayden[1]

HADDON Heights, New Jersey, has the distinction of having the consummate baby boomer as one of its citizens. Kathleen Casey Wilkins is the U.S.A.'s original baby boomer.

Money magazine reported, "She wouldn't have wanted to have been born in another time."[2] Wilkins was born at one second after midnight, January 1, 1946. Following on her heels were 76 million people between the years of 1946 and 1964. They were all called "baby boomers" because of the explosive number of births in that time period.

Wilkins is now the mother of two daughters: Ann, 17, and Jennifer, 15. She concedes that she does fit some of the stereotypes of her generation. She works out three times a week, plays tennis, drives a 1985 Mercedes-Benz, avoids red meat, travels to Europe, owns a food processor and is working toward a master's degree in business administration.

DESCRIBING AVERAGE BOOMERS

Approximately 51.2 percent of the United States' 247.9 million people are women. The average United States citizen then, according to the May 15, 1989 issue of *USA TODAY*, is a married woman, age 32, who owns two TVs and an eight-year-old car, and makes less than $20,000 a year at a white-collar job she commutes to from suburbia.[3] That's the reverse of 50 years ago when the average American was a 29-year-old male working at a factory job in the city.

The *American Demographics* magazine of June 1989 says that Jane Doe—today's average American woman—"is not June Cleaver [of the 'Leave It to Beaver' TV show years ago]. She is more like Roseanne Barr [the outspoken character on the current TV show 'Roseanne']."[4]

Compared with her mother, Jane is more mobile, better educated, more likely to work outside the home, more apt to own a house, and she will live years longer than her mother.

At 5'4" and 143 pounds, Jane is overweight and usually dieting. She also has 1.8 children. Her house could sell for $84,000, and she has a TV, VCR or stereo on 11 hours a day. Once home from her job, Jane faces 3.5 hours of housework and child care. And she makes six phone calls a day.

But *American Demographics* adds, Jane's life is also more harried. It costs her $140,000 to raise a child. She is more likely to divorce (a 50 percent chance). She'll move 11 times during her life, and she'll be victimized by crime three times. This portrait of Jane Doe is drawn from U.S. Government statistics and from an almanac of American people.[5]

COMPARING THE GENERATIONS

To understand this generation requires a comparison with the other smaller generations in our society. Pluralism exists in the United States, not only in regional, ethnic and religious distinctives, but in our very generational spread as well. As many as four generations coexist in our culture right now. Marketers and the media recognize the necessity of understanding the differentials between generations.

The Survivor Generation

Survivors are the grandparents of baby boomers. Raised during the years of World War I, the Great Depression and World War II, the grandparents came out with the basic instinct of survival. This generation survived the most harsh cultural and societal conditions; and yet they brought about a very productive society.

The Consumer Generation

This generalized term, "the consumer generation," characterizes the parents of baby boomers. These people were the first to discover time payments and mortgages under the GI Bill of Rights. And thanks to the weakened conditions of England, Australia, New Zealand, Japan and Germany following World War II, this generation experienced the greatest economic and industrial expansion in the history of civilization, as the United States industrial base enjoyed unprecedented growth and development.

Consequently, this generation tends to be more impressed with its purchasing power than boomers are. This consumer generation has also profited greatly because of the baby boom, through the accelerated values and prices of their homes and the increased purchasing power of their dollars.

In addition, this generation has been the predominant funding base for most Christian organizations for several decades. Even now, most of the funding of the Church comes from people 55 and over. Not surprisingly then, the predominant cultural mentality within the Church, with few exceptions, is that of the consumer generation.

Yet, this is also the generation that began the slide away from church life.

Baby Boomers

Those 76 million or so baby boomers are now between 25 and 43 years of age. The many subgroups in this generation indicate that we aren't entirely as homogeneous as many would think. Our reaction to the Vietnam War quickly reveals this truth. The sons of America's blue-collar workers ended up fighting this war while those of us who were children of middle-class families avoided the war by attending universities.

Then too, older boomers have profited from the inflation swing of 1970. And they also began using drugs and

---

Unifying our outlook and attitude is the fact that we all share a common cultural experience.

---

indulging in sexual experimentation. But younger boomers found their dollars shrinking before they could get them and watched the mythic drug culture turn sour on them.

Yet for all our differences, this generation still possesses a great deal of homogeneity. As a group, we remain incredibly optimistic, very open to spiritual experience and are devoted to the rock culture of Mick Jagger and Paul McCartney.

A *Newsweek* magazine columnist, while recognizing our generation's rather consistent outlook on life, was, however, somewhat less than charitable in describing it. For some, our "'you-cannot-experience-what-we've-experienced' attitude is most frustrating, making [our] entire generation appear insufferably 'self-possessed.'"6

Unifying our outlook and attitude is the fact that we all share a common cultural experience. Most of our generation remember the days of the Berkeley free speech riots and the Kent State shootings by national guardsmen—memories which still bring anger. Psychedelia, Jefferson Airplane, marijuana, Jimi Hendrix, the Rolling Stones and

Mustang convertibles all ring familiar to the generation coming of age in that era.

The immortal words of John F. Kennedy, "Ask not what your country can do for you; ask what you can do for your country"[7] are etched on the hearts and minds of most baby boomers, along with Martin Luther King, Jr.'s dream and the first appearance of the Beatles on the "Ed Sullivan Show."

Undoubtedly, the most common reference point for any boomer is the assassination of President John F. Kennedy. In conversations with people my age, the conversation invariably rolls around to: Where were you when Kennedy was killed?

At the time, I was at my eighth grade band practice when our principal's voice came over the school intercom, announcing that our president, John F. Kennedy, had just been assassinated, that we now had a new president, Lyndon B. Johnson, and that school would be dismissed for the rest of the day.

The current TV show "thirtysomething" is an apt characterization of this generation of baby boomers. We thirty somethings do stand out as unique. Specifically, what makes us so special? Here's some reasons:

- We're the first generation to be raised, by and large, with absentee fathers.
- We're also the first generation whose grandparents had no significant input in terms of life preparation and wage-earning skills.
- We're the most educated generation in history.
- We were raised in extreme affluence, with opportunities unimaginable to our parents.
- We came into childhood and adolescence at the time of the greatest economic expansion in world history.

- We're the first generation with less purchasing power than our parents at each stage in adulthood.
- We're the first generation who can't afford what we've always had.
- We're the first generation raised under the near-constant threat of nuclear war.
- We're the first generation to be reared with television as a significant parenting tool.

Baby Buster Generation

Baby busters are the children of baby boomers. They tend to be far more conservative than their immediate elders, disenfranchised from the Church world and—though this generation ought to be the most optimistic—unwaveringly pessimistic.

Yet the positive economic outlook for their lives is unprecedented. Two years ago colleges graduated only 8 percent more graduates while the job market had room for 25 percent. Still, this generation will probably go to the grave pessimistic, because they have reaped the havoc created by the unwholesome experimentation of their boomer parents.

RELATING TO BOOMERS

The Church in the 1990s will find itself at a crossroads, and its ability to include the baby boomer generation will set its course. George Barna of the Barna Research Group in the *National & International Religion Report,* discusses seven major trends facing the Church at the end of this century and states that the most significant opportunity for growth has to do with the aging baby boomers:

Three aspects that emerge from survey research suggest that the baby boomers will be the most important source of church growth in the coming decade. First, realize that this segment, as a whole, will reach the age cohort at which life begins to stabilize (job, housing, family, finances), and attachment to traditional values and institutions become more likely. To many people in the 30-50 age bracket, church membership is a symbol of belonging, a way of becoming an accepted and ingrained part of the community.

Second, adults in the baby-boom cohort have apparently "burned out" on popular culture to the extent that religion is now assuming a more important place in their lives. Since 1982, the proportion of adults who claim that religion is "very important" and returned to church has jumped nearly 20 percent—with much of that increase a result of the renewed interest in religion among baby boomers.[8]

So how will the Church relate to the Kathleen Wilkinses and the Jane Does of the 1990s? If their spiritual legacy is still up for grabs, and if they are—as George Barna reports—returning to church with a renewed interest in religion, then what the Church does about this generation could be the question of this decade.

The tension can be felt in any denomination today. Why? Because, for the most part, American Christianity is dominated by our parents' generation—the consumer generation—that disdains the experience of the 1960s. And we boomers, despite our desire to return to a real spiritual experience, are unable to relate to a church culture dominated by our parents. Ironically, though only one generation apart chronologically, these two generations are light years apart culturally.

So even though boomers are returning to church in surprising numbers, you may not find any coming to your church, simply because it may be a model of church life we can't relate to. Yes, boomers are beginning to try churches, but we are finding few that we will give ourselves to in a

---

American Christianity is dominated by our parents' generation. And we boomers, despite our desire to return to a real spiritual experience, are unable to relate to a church culture dominated by our parents.

---

committed way. This increase in church attendance without a correspondingly positive attitude toward religion is evidence of a significant problem that we will look at in greater detail later.

Yet unless you're a boomer, you will find it hard to realize what a big leap it is for us to jump into traditional forms of worship and church that worked well before the 1960s. But must the leap be so great? Should it be? Hopefully not.

Jack Simms, a nationally recognized authority on baby boomer mentality, gives a popular lecture with the title, "Why Are These People Smiling? Because They Don't Have to Go to Church Anymore." Then, almost in contradiction to this title, he states that boomers are returning to church—to certain churches, at least—in surprising numbers.

But why are boomers open to attending some churches and not others. Simms lists 10 traits common to those churches that are reaching baby boomers for Christ:

1. They are open to a spiritual experience.
2. Their Bible teaching stresses practical living.
3. They place a healthy emphasis on relationships.
4. They have fewer titles and less formality.
5. They understand the new family in America.
6. They share their faith by what they say and do.
7. They recognize the ability of women.
8. They place an emphasis on worship.
9. They have a high tolerance for diversity.
10. They are action-oriented.[9]

Simms advises visiting a church, any church, even your own church, and rating it on a scale of 1-10 in each of the 10 categories.

If the score is	Then
65% or less	The church needs dramatic improvement.
66% to 80%	The church is not doing badly.
81% or more	Folks will miss the NFL pregame show and arrive 30 minutes early to get a parking spot.

UNDERSTANDING THE BOOMER BELIEF SYSTEM

In this book, I will key in on nine essential understandings for reaching baby boomers. The churches in the 1990s most able to respond effectively to my generation will be those that understand best these nine aspects of the boomer belief system:

Understanding No. 1: Baby boomers are not belongers.
We are great participants, but not very good belongers. Church membership will need to be downplayed and replaced with terms and experiences that emphasize participation.

Understanding No. 2: Boomers are noninstitutional.
We are very low on denominational loyalty. So, due to heavy demands on our time, we will most likely commit to a local nondenominational church rather than drive a longer distance to a church of our own denomination.

It is reported that suburban Americans in 1991 will have 17 percent less free time per household, due to commuting, raising children and so on. These suburbanites will judge the Church by how we in the Church value their time. If we think that attending three services a week is a measure of spirituality, we will miss this generation.

By and large, both boomer parents work and haul kids to Little League, basketball practice, day care and so on. They don't have time to attend three services a week, and they will not tolerate any guilt trips or put up with any suggestions that they are being substandard Christians by not attending all services.

Understanding No. 3: Boomers are experience oriented.
They have experienced everything from Silly Putty to the LSD craze to stereo mania. Boomers purchase stereos for the sheer experience of listening to the spectrum of sound frequencies.

Understanding No. 4: We boomers are extremely pragmatic in our sermon tastes.
Ministers will need to make their "take-away points" very clear and early in their messages.

Understanding No. 5: Boomers believe women need to be represented in leadership.

This generation will judge the Church's morality by the participation of women. The large preponderance of single women in this generation has influenced men at least on the surface level. Where women are not recognized in leadership positions, those congregations will be judged to be morally invalid in the hearts of some and at least a little out-of-touch in the hearts of others.

Understanding No. 6: Boomers expect that the contribution of singles will be celebrated and accepted.

Every sermon illustration and metaphor will have to be relevant to both marrieds and singles. It is projected that by 1992 a full 50 percent of adults in America will be single.

Understanding No. 7: Boomers believe the high level of dysfunctionality of this group needs to be faced.

Churches in the 1990s that minister to baby boomers will have to be comfortable with dysfunction. Instances of herpes, homosexuality, AIDS and the fact that one-fourth of these women have been sexually abused by the time they reach adulthood will put increasing pressure on the Church for relevant support groups. A great need will exist for expertise in the area of counseling and for skill on the part of preaching ministries to deal sensitively with very painful issues and hurting people.

Understanding No. 8: Boomers will applaud innovation.

We see a need for diversity expressed with multiple options—sometimes just for the simple reason of being innovative. Multiple service times, ranging from Friday and Saturday nights to multiple times on Sundays, as well as a wide variety of face-to-face small group opportunities, will be necessary in order to appeal to the baby boomers. Innovation may have appeal, just because it's innovative.

Understanding No. 9: Boomers have a sense of destiny.

We possess an uncanny belief in our ability to make the world better. We are simply awaiting the leadership and occasions to ignite us to action. Perhaps it will be a mid-life action, but it is effective all the same.

STRATEGIZING OUR MODUS OPERANDI

Is it legitimate to address deliberately a particular segment of our population? My response to that question is, "Of course! Every missionary targets his audience."

Every missionary who goes into an unchurched situation evaluates the cultural distinctions to discover ways to communicate to that world. Most reports suggest that the second significant opportunity for church growth in our decade is the Hispanic Church. The first opportunity is reaching baby boomers. Very specialized, specific approaches will be required to reach each group.

Pluralism is a great challenge to the Church in our American culture. The marketing mania of our society has caused our culture to be divided into ever-smaller segments. Each has its own language, and each expects to be catered to. This segmentation process will make our task easier if we in the Church learn to embrace it and accept it is a factor in our ministry.

The apostle Paul recognized the need to respond to multilayers in the societies he reached. In 1 Corinthians 9:19-23, Paul writes to the Church of Corinth describing his modus operandi (MO):

> Though I am free and belong to no man, I make myself a slave to everyone, to win as many as possible. To the Jews I became like a Jew, to win the Jews.
>
> To those under the law I became like one under the law (though I myself am not under the law), so as to win those under the law. To those not having the law I became like one not having the law (though I am not free from God's law but am under Christ's law), so as to win those not having the law.
>
> To the weak I became weak, to win the weak. I have become all things to all men so that by all possible means I might save some. I do all this for the sake of the gospel, that I may share in its blessings.

These three concepts can be gleaned from the apostle's strategy for formatting his ministry:

1. Intelligibility,

2. Sensitivity,

3. Integrity,

Intelligibility

Presentation of the gospel demands *intelligibility.* The whole purpose of the apostle's comments in 1 Corinthians 9-14 is to make certain that the gospel is intelligible. The tongues-speaking of the Corinthians was creating confusion and causing the message to be blurred and unintelligent.

The very essence of ministry, as described in these chapters, is to go to great lengths to make certain that the incarnation principle of Jesus—God making Himself known in the flesh—is continued in the Church. We accomplish this purpose when we make the gospel intelligible to the unchurched. Intelligibility, then, is the very means of ministry.

Some sociologists suggest that we now have a new generation birthed every five years. Our society is belching out new sets of values, new sets of expectations and common experiences at a mind-boggling rate. We really do find ourselves with the challenging task of continuing to be intelligible.

Intelligibility takes a great deal of effort. It means pausing to examine our communication to see if we are communicating clearly in ways that people can understand. To make this effort is necessary, for, in not attempting to be intelligible, we risk having our message fall on deaf ears.

When I met Christ, having never attended church, I couldn't understand the *King James Version* (*KJV*) of the Bible. All those "thees" and "thous" of the *KJV* really tripped me up. I might just be a slow case, but that translation itself didn't communicate well to me. After several years, someone handed me a *Living New Testament*. Then for the first time, I was able to understand the Bible.

The very music in some churches I attended—the archaic hymns, the slow pace of the services, the nonparticipation—turned me off. But somewhere along the way, I landed in a church which was expressive in both praise and worship. They used a guitar from time to time, and the music had a good rhythm to it.

At that time we called such music "Spirit-filled." It probably was, but, as much as anything else, it fitted my particular taste in music with a nice rhythm and beat to it. In an adventuresome expression of worship, I welcomed the opportunity to have personal experiences that were biblically sound, but nonetheless mine.

Sensitivity

All who communicate through the spoken word need to have *sensitivity* toward the feelings and needs of their listeners.

Recently, I cringed as I listened to a speaker in a seminar that dealt with issues of divorce and remarriage. He pled with the pastors at the seminar never to marry people who had been divorced. He even went so far as to have them stand up and take a pledge that they would never do such a thing.

However, when it came time to stand up, I couldn't. First, I don't believe his premise is biblical. Second, I thought the guy was totally out of touch. And third, it obviously had been quite some time since he had led an unchurched person to Christ.

I glanced around the room. Two of us didn't stand up. And both of us, interestingly enough, were 10 to 15 years younger than the rest of the men and women in that room. The two of us glanced at one another as if to say, "He doesn't understand our world, does he?"

It's very difficult to minister to a generation in which so many have had abortions, been divorced and remarried, and may even be struggling with all varieties of addiction—drug, alcohol, sexual and so on. Ministering to such a flock requires a great deal of sensitivity.

Many of my friends who struggle with going back to church have been unable to see the real caring and loving people that I've grown to know in the Church, simply because the communication style of some pastors comes across insensitively. I know few people in the Church who would reject a divorced man or woman, yet I do know that, by some of our preaching expressions, we keep people at arm's length. And they feel unsafe in a place which should be the safest place they can find—the fellowship circle of God's people.

Integrity

> Do you not know that in a race all the runners run, but only one gets the prize? Run in such a way as to get the prize. Everyone who competes in the games goes into strict training. They do it to get a crown that will not last; but we do it to get a crown that will last forever.
>
> Therefore, I do not run like a man running aimlessly; I do not fight like a man beating the air. No, I beat my body and make it my slave so that after I have preached to others, I myself will not be disqualified for the prize (1 Cor. 9:24-27).

The third ingredient in Paul's mission strategy was *integrity*. Integrity has to do with substance that makes style meaningful and eternal. I recently had the privilege of speaking at a leader's seminar. After my presentation, we discussed together the necessity for evangelism and church life that is intelligible, sensitive and encouraging.

In the course of our discussion, one of the leaders asked me, "In our attempts to be sensitive and intelligible, don't we run the risk of compromising the gospel message?"

Thinking for a moment, I answered yes.

Yes, we do run the risk of compromise when we appeal to the sensitivity of others. We at least run the risk of imbalances. So the challenge to be in balance is ever before us if reaching the unchurched is of concern to us.

But the integrity of our lives and the integrity of the message of the gospel are essential to authentic biblical communication. In attempting to be heard by boomers, we must hold fast to the integrity of orthodox beliefs and practices taught in the Scriptures. I conclude that it is possible to do so.

NICHING OUR APPEAL

Evangelism must be niched more than ever in the '90s. Any suburban city in America contains as many as six or seven strata of different kinds of people to be reached. In a book entitled, *The Clustering of America,* this point is brought home strongly. The author, Michael J. Weiss, suggests that as many as 40 neighborhood types exist. In fact, Weiss even suggests that the "average American" is a myth; no average American exists. He challenges marketers and government officials to realize that communications links exist to all these strata in society.

If that's the case, niching—targeting specific groups—is even more vital to churches than it is to businesses. I've been involved in a number of pioneer church projects— starting new churches—over the years. And I'm convinced that the vast majority of them failed for the simple reason that we didn't target our audience precisely enough. We haven't played the odds and appealed to the baby boomer generation consistently.

RETURNING TO CHURCH, IF—

Believe me, we thirty something folks are ready to return to church. Our kids are causing us to come back. Every time we look into their big eyes and hear the questions about God, we move closer. So indeed, the culture of the baby boomer is very, very open to spiritual reality—if presented in terms we will feel "at home" with.

But we are fearful as we go back to church that we'll encounter the same irrelevant, distasteful experiences we remember from our youth: dank basements of Sunday School rooms with concrete walls, cheerless music and an environment that promises relationships, but leaves everyone with nothing more than an indifferent handshake after the service.

If I have a dream, it is this: that churches in America's cities will seek to appeal to the baby boomer generation—a generation that has been unable to relate to traditional forms. Several practical considerations might help us. Let's consider them next.

Notes
1. Tom Hayden, "Decade Shock," *Newsweek*, September 5, 1988, p. 14
2. "Nationline," *USA Today*, January 1, 1988.
3. "Average U.S. Citizen: Married Woman 32," *USA Today*, May 15 1989, p. 3-A.
4. Ibid.
5. "Monday," *USA Today*, May 15, 1989, p. 3-A.
6. "Will We Ever Get over the Sixties?" *Newsweek*, September 5, 1988.
7. John F. Kennedy, "Inaugural Address," January 20, 1961.
8. George Barna, "Seven Trends Facing the Church in 1988 and Beyond," *National & International Religion Report*, 1988, p. 3.
9. Jack Simms, "Why Are These People Smiling? Because They Don't Have to Go to Church Anymore," Lecture at Fuller Theological Seminary, Pasadena, California, (n.d.).

2

BUT WILL THEY
JOIN OUR CHURCH?

*"Why don't these people become
members like I did?"*
—Church Council Member

A Baby Boomer Encounter

On a recent flight from Seattle to Denver, I sat next to a successful black engineer. He was in his early 40s—born between 1946 and 1964—which qualified him as a baby boomer. We were on a DC-10 en route to Denver, just one week after the crash of another ill-fated DC-10 over Iowa that had the same flight schedule and number. Knowledge of that disquieting similarity meant our plane was loaded with people who were all a little tense and nervous.

My seat companion and I were both dressed casually. He was ready to play tennis at the conference site as soon as the plane touched down. I said that my immediate plan was to sleep. Getting up at 5:00 A.M. to catch a plane is not my usual practice. As our plane passed over Oregon, he told me about his job. Though now very successful, he had stayed in the urban black community in which he had grown up.

Finally, as he pushed his glasses back up the bridge of his nose and leaned back in his seat, he asked me the big question: "And what do you do?"

I swallowed deeply. "I hate to tell you this, but I'm a pastor," I responded.

His startled expression spoke louder than his tone of voice could ever have. The look on his face said, "A what?!"

To lighten things up a bit, I hastened to add, "Yes, I'm a pastor, and I write a little bit also. But come on! I won't give you some kind of religious disease!"

Glancing at the person to the engineer's right, who was also staring at me now, I leaned forward and said, "Yes, that's right. I'm a minister—you know, a pastor."

Not willing to leave it at that, the engineer turned toward me and said earnestly: "You are? You know, I grew up in church. In fact, my dad was a deacon. I've actually been thinking about coming back to church."

"Gee, that's great! But why, may I ask?"

In asking him why, I tried not to show that my interest in his story might have a deeper motive. For I was concerned that—without scaring him away—I might have an opportunity to answer any questions this young man might have about Jesus Christ.

"Well, my daughters keep asking me to go," he replied. "Last week, my youngest asked me to go to the Catholic Church with her and her friend, but I grew up a Baptist."

He explained further, his face registering mild pain as he recalled past events in his life: "Sure it [church] was good for me. But after I came back from 'Nam, I just never got started going to church again. I went through a lot of hell too: a busted marriage, alcoholism, scrambling my brains for a few years on women.

"And now I'm a dad. I have a couple of girls in grade school."

As he glanced down the aisle, watching the stewardess push the food cart toward us, he asked, "Got any advice for me? What church can I go to where I'll understand all that? My daughter will like it; she likes church. I would go if I could just get something out of it. But I remember everything being so serious. Do you think I could handle it again?"

As the conversation wound down, I suggested a couple of congregations in the area where he lived. I assured him that, even though we talked about being against drugs, alcohol, divorce and so on, the Christians in those churches really would love him, regardless of the mistakes he had made. And certainly, his kids deserved to know the Lord.

I know my young engineer friend probably exemplifies many thousands in our baby boomer generation. He's beginning a serious spiritual assessment of his life. For some time he had thought church was irrelevant, had gone through bouts of addiction and felt certain that the Church would reject him as a result.

My prayer is that he will find somewhere to attend where they will immediately befriend him to make his transition easier. But what will it take for my black engineer friend and other boomers like him to sign up on the church roll? Let's try to find out.

REMEMBER WOODSTOCK

But first, test yourself with this quiz. We'll grade you in a moment.

- First question: What is Mr. Yasgur's farm in upstate New York famous for?
- Second question: What was the location of a raucous, orgylike celebration of rock 'n' roll music, where 500,000 young people gathered for several days in the summer of 1969?

If, in answer to the first question, you said Yasgur's farm was the site of the famous concert, known as Woodstock, you were right. If you said Woodstock, New York, in answer to the second question, you were right again.

In 1989, 20 years later, the legend of Woodstock reared its head again. This unusual event's folklore graced the covers of nearly every major news magazine in the country. VH-1 and MTV music cable channels ran almost three months of special programs and flashbacks to this event.

Madison Avenue likewise capitalized on the appeal of this legendary happening. Yet it was more than just a bunch of hype. For, to our generation, the lore of Woodstock is almost a folk theology.

Every generation has its own folklore. Those common experiences that shape a generation's identity comprise the makeup of those identities. Through a twist of fate, some generations end up with a stronger lore than others. We boomers are one of those generations blessed with an intense folklore.

The folklore of my mother's generation included legendary bathtub gin, the stock market crash, the Great Depression, soup lines and kitchens, and World War II—the war after the war that was to end all wars. Most of Mom's friends told me stories about deprivation and creative survival. What child of parents in my parents' age-group hasn't heard stories about persons who soled their shoes with cardboard and stuffed them with newsprint to make them last longer, because they couldn't afford new ones?

I thought for a long time, until I went to college, that I alone grew up as the child of uniquely deprived folks. But, one afternoon, when our class discussed the impact of the Great Depression on the American psyche, I discovered that nearly every kid in the class had heard stories similar to mine. Their folks too had endured that era of deprivation and had also admonished them with the same exhortation to "be thankful" for how much they had.

Tales echoed throughout the classroom that day of people eating dandelions out of the yard, feasting on a rabbit that had been hit by a car or playing ball with a stick, because no one could afford a real bat. And none of us boomer students ever quite figured out how our parents got so enthused about a game called "kick-the-can," though they still speak of it today as one of the favorite pastimes of their childhood.

Life experiences shape us and our theological outlook as well; our felt needs have a great deal to do with making us who we are. To be sure then, all the folklore of my parents' generation greatly impacted their worldview.

We baby boomers aren't coming to church to become members. We're coming to experience something. Yes, even to get something. What we're hoping for is some kind, human touch...

And my generation is no different. The average baby boomer was eight when the first band fired up its deafening amplifiers in Yasgur's pastures. The Vietnam War was raging, and rock 'n' roll became our avenue of releasing frustration, just as Woodstock became this generation's vision of what it believed the future should hold for them.

So 20 years later, some recalled the Woodstock event with almost religious awe. Others couldn't imagine why all the fuss about rolling around in the rain and mud for several days in 1969. Strangely enough, the myth records no arrests at all for crime. Nor was there any violence either. "Free love" filled the grounds. And illegal drugs abounded everywhere. A sense of unity and destiny prevailed at Woodstock, and amazingly the experience was felt far beyond those who were there.

And the myth of Woodstock still lingers. Though its detractors are justified for the most part, Woodstock continues to strike a common chord of fond remembrance for most baby boomers. For us, Woodstock proved that religious citadels and stained glass weren't necessary in order to have a "religious experience" of unimaginable proportions. Yet at Woodstock, there were no laws, no priests, no Bibles—just a lot of music, mud, drugs, sex and people.

From that powerful experience emerged the theology of Woodstock: human love and unity, equality, respect, an appreciation for differences, and a total abandonment to celebration. People needed and helped each other; camaraderies were formed. For those present, Woodstock was a fantasy dreamworld for a few, mesmerizing days.

Secretly, I think we thirty something folks believe that the myth of Woodstock is what the Church, in a certain sense, ought to emulate. Church ought to be celebrative, informal and spontaneous. People sharing and helping each other should not only be an expectation, but a reality.

The theology of Woodstock is the dream of a generation. We hope it is possible to have religion without formal titles and without unnecessary rules. Isn't there some place where people simply need each other for survival? Isn't there a place where each individual is important and respected? Can't I know God as a person? Isn't it possible for us humans to relate to God without all those official channels?

The Church's failure to appreciate the impact of Woodstock could cause it to miss a wonderful opportunity in communicating the gospel intelligibly to an entire generation.

Boomers and Church Membership

So why won't these people become members? I asked myself this question a hundred times before I finally understood why. Yet the answer is simple: *baby boomers are nonjoiners.*

We may attend your church, and if we do we're likely to be more committed than our disinterest in signing the church roster may indicate. But give us our anonymity, please—at least for the moment. Don't get impatient if we aren't ready to sign on the dotted line for some time.

I remember the first time I visited a church. These questions raced through my mind:

- Will they make me stand up and introduce myself?
- Are they going to grab me to make me a member right off?

For me, these were more than mere questions; they were the fears of a deep, primordial instinct to survive.

We baby boomers aren't coming to church to become members. We're coming to *experience* something. Yes, even to *get* something. What we're hoping for is some kind, human touch in these churches we're checking out. So, getting us on your membership roll could prove quite an exciting challenge for you.

At Eastside Church, we have tried at least 10 different approaches to membership. Some of them have worked, but only for short seasons. For our congregation, like other boomer congregations, has rarely had much enthusiasm about signing up on our church's roster.

From our experience, I have concluded that this process of acquiring members is one that requires constant evaluation and updating. In the 1990s, church leaders will face continuing struggles and challenges as they seek to devise strategies for building their memberships. But any successful strategy involving boomers will include at least these two essential elements:

- Offer participation, not just membership, and
- Emphasize the individual, not the institution.

Offer Participation, Not Just Membership

One afternoon, our ministry team and I tried to resolve the membership issue once and for all. By now, we were several thousand strong, we were stable, we had a large amount of assets, and our budget was consistently in seven figures—yet we didn't have very many members.

Dave spoke first. "I just don't understand why these people can't become members. I think you ought to require it before they can serve as workers in this church."

Dorothy, our Children's Church worker, added her comment: "Yeah, right—that ought to cut our work force by about 90 percent."

Mike chimed in. "Who wants to become a member anyway? Check that list. See if I'm on it."

Lucky checked the list before him. What he discovered was hilarious. As he glanced down the list, not only were Mike and Carmen's names absent (those of my assistant pastor and his wife), but Debbie's name and mine were also conspicuously absent!

Chagrined and embarrassed, I hastened to assure everybody there that it was simply an oversight; that Debbie and I were very committed to this church. Everyone laughed.

"Okay," I broke in, "how do we deal with this issue of membership? Frankly, I'm tired of holding these membership classes, having about 40 people attend, speaking for two hours, and then seeing only two or three become members. It's kind of embarrassing to have them stand up at the end of a service when there are only three of them."

"Maybe it's the word 'member,'" someone suggested.

I don't know who came up with that great bit of insight, but it caught my ear. I thought: *Ah, ha! That's it! The term "member" is what's scaring them off!*

Thirty something folks are fearful of being just another name on another long list. *We want to be participants. We want to be part of something meaningful.* Conversely, membership somehow carries with it the connotation of giving up some freedoms. Perhaps it also has to do with the fear of being lost in the masses.

Who knows? Maybe this was etched in our psyches when we had to attend overcrowded junior highs and high schools. When the lines at theaters swelled, we wanted to be more than just another face in the crowd.

I felt there had to be a solution, however, for we certainly do value the obvious importance of commitment. None of us doubted that an expressed commitment to the "company of believers" is an essential part of spiritual maturity. Any sane person knows that no congregation will work without committed people—commitment which is recognized by church attendance, participation and giving.

As I leaned back in my chair, pondering the matter, Betsy asked: "Well, Doug, maybe our people are all like you. I mean, you're the typical boomer. Would you belong to a church?"

I responded: "Well, yes, of course I would, but I probably wouldn't become a member."

We decided then that the problem was one of terminology. By the end of our search for a solution, it was decided to design a course, titled "Church 101." It's a beginning course on church life, describing our denominational affiliation, our philosophy and our values as a church. We learn how to be a part of a church and provide an opportunity for people to become participants in our church rather than mere members.

Participants are encouraged to work in a volunteer capacity for at least six months and must agree to be givers. Essentially, a participant is the same as a member in the traditional sense, but the term "participant" simply imparts a pleasanter connotation to the hearer's ears than does "member."

After all, far more is involved in the concept of participating, giving and committing one's life to walk in biblical precepts with a company of believers than in one's merely signing a membership roll. I would suggest, therefore, that any church, aspiring to attract significant numbers of boomers, handle the term "member" with care. So boomers will get their expectations straight, define "member" in such a way that it deals with participatory terms.

Meanwhile, be patient with boomers concerning the membership process. Eventually we'll come around, though probably later than you would wish. But if you concentrate on getting boomers to undertake ministry tasks before you ask them to sign anything, they will be more apt to hang around.

EMPHASIZE THE INDIVIDUAL, NOT THE INSTITUTION

Step two in developing a boomer sensitivity to Christ and His Body is a willingness to emphasize the individual over the institution. Such an emphasis involves (a) replacing traditionalism with informality and casualness and (b) stressing relationships rather than structure and creeds.

Celebrate Informality

We boomers aren't just nonjoiners; we are paranoid about formality. We don't care for church institutions. In fact, we would like to tear your pretentious structures down and start over with something more "spontaneous."

Formality is phony as far as most of us are concerned. To us, casual is human. Genuine churches ought to be highly human in the boomer's mind. By all means, don't appear formal to us. We can't handle that. What we are searching for when we attend church is informality with meaning.

What we are saying is that even though we boomers are coming back to church, we aren't willing to attend formalized institutions. "Traditional" is a bad word to us. But "stability" is not. Stable congregations who build on a caring environment that's heavy on the personal touch and participation will have ample opportunities to see people who are thirty something join their ranks.

Jeans in the Pew

The TV sitcom, "thirtysomething," won't be able to stick to its name much longer, because we will turn forty something in the 1990s. But whether we are thirty something or turn forty something, we're still the Levi 501s generation. We may require the bigger-bottom variety as we age, but we're still wearing Levi's.

We'll probably remain jeans-wearing people too. Why? Because they're comfortable. And they're also a commentary on casualness.

David Letterman, the late-night talk show host, regularly wears jeans with a double-breasted suit jacket. Even in the business world, I see this combo a lot. And what is being said by those who wear it?

Well, here's my analysis: Okay, so you got me into this church scenario, but I'm letting you know I don't like it when it's stuffy and formal. There's a real individual inside these Levi's. So don't judge me for what I'm wearing; appreciate me for who I am.

High Tech, High Touch

That means, if you're a pastor, be very casual and, above all, human. We don't want you hiding out of reach, aloof and distant. We'd like you to touch us with your humanity. Tell us about your failures and your fears and help us baby boomers to know there's some hope for our fears and failures.

You see, fast-growing technology has made a lot of us feel faceless and nameless. Our culture's fixation with efficiency has caused us to feel that we are of secondary importance as persons. We feel we are but appendages to the machinery that drives our quest for the techno-perfect world.

John Naisbitt, who authored *Megatrends*, informs us that a high-tech world creates the need for high touch. High touch is required for any congregation to become a healing community. A congregation centering on a relational contact with God will be an oasis in the desert in which baby boomers have grown up. Formal religion seems like more of the same faceless world to us.

The questions we want to ask church leaders are:

- Are you a person?
- Can we be persons around you?

We have grown up in the techno-revolution. Thirty something people have survived overcrowded school systems. In those shell-shocked education systems that rarely had the time or a caring attitude to know us as people, we were mere numbers and statistics.

The evening fare of television is filled with shows that appeal to America's hunger for authentic relationships. Programs like "The Cosby Show," "Family Ties" and "Cheers" all emphasize the relational ties between their characters. According to its theme song, Cheers is the bar in Boston where you can go and "everyone knows your name."

We call the small-group meetings in our congregation face-to-face groups. I wish I could say the vast majority of people in our congregation are in these small groups. They aren't, but providing the opportunity for small-group interaction is essential nevertheless.

A multitude of reasons explain why thirty something boomers are dropping back into church in growing numbers. One reason is: *We expect to find a high-touch environment where people are genuinely interested in us as persons. We also hope to find a God we can know on a personal level and who will know us.*

A high-touch, relationally friendly church environment isn't easy for either a large or a small church to provide, as our entire culture has become so habituated to a depersonalized world. The phone company may demonstrate it easily in their reach-out-and-touch-someone ads. But in real life, it's tough. To reach out and touch someone takes incredible effort and genuine caring.

To reach out and touch baby boomers, everything from pulpit messages to the church's weekly bulletin will need to stress: *God can be known personally by you, and you are more important to Him—and to us—than this church's existence.*

We boomers look to you with hungry hearts, because this high-tech world is so toxic and so all-consuming.

Because it has nearly suffocated us, do allow us to be human around you.

Shed Those Formal Titles

High touch means putting a "face" on life—that is, using your first name—instead of a Mr., Ms. or Mrs.—and a handshake in a transaction. We boomers are title-haters, so drop the churchy titles, please. And forget about your degrees. We really don't care about them either.

One Saturday morning, five of us from Eastside Church sat around our living room. With the exception of one individual, we were all in the thirty-to-forty something category. We all had committed a great deal of time and effort to our church, and it had become apparent to us that our growing church needed to have a more recognized leadership. So our task was to determine how we could develop such leadership in our church.

I said to my friends, "We have a deep need to have recognized leadership in this church other than myself. We've grown by 200 people these past two months, and already there are a number of pastoral care needs that neither I nor my assistant will be able to get to. I think we need to have something like an eldership."

Gordon chimed in. "No way will you call me an elder? I've been through that. I don't want everybody putting me on some sort of pedestal or making me out to be some kind of a heavy."

Dave, who was about 10 years older than the rest of us, then jumped in: "Now, I've been raised in church all my life. I'm sick of this elder stuff."

I had to admit that I agreed with them, so I forged ahead: "You know, you guys are right. I don't like being called 'reverend' either. Our congregation is likely to laugh at us anyway if we come up with an elder scenario. Many of them have come out of churches where they didn't appreciate that kind of thing.

"So what are we going to do?"

Larry said, "Well, do you have to call us anything? Can't we just, you know, be people there to help?"

"Well, we have to indicate that we have some sort of structure, don't you think?" I countered.

"You can have all kinds of structure. Just don't call us anything, especially 'elders,'" begged Larry.

Joe interjected, "Besides that, doesn't the Bible suggest that an elder should have gray hair. We don't have gray hair."

It was brought home to me again that morning that the kind of environment we had created was really evolving into one quite different from anything I'd previously experienced in church leadership. Most churches where I'd attended, the elders were clearly identified, and everyone appreciated it. Perhaps they didn't always understand what being an elder meant, but it was appreciated, all the same.

At first, we just called our pastoral care group "the leadership." Eventually, this group became "volunteer pastors" and, on some occasions, "the ministry team." Informality was "in." After all, if I was just, plain Doug, why did they have to be formal somebodies?

So if you don't use Elder This and Reverend That in your church, all the better. One of the hardest tasks for me to do is to sign anything with a "reverend" before my name, though my hesitancy to do so is not based upon humility. I just don't like formality any more than my peers do. For you to call me "Doug" is just fine, maybe even "Pastor Doug." But I really prefer "Doug."

My wife, Debbie, doesn't like the formal title of "reverend" either—but for another reason. She says, "You're not reverent enough to be called 'reverend.'"

Yes, we boomers do ask you to celebrate your informality with us and, by all means, tell us your name. I'm just Doug. Won't you be a face with a name too? We hope so. If not, we boomers will find a church where people are faces with names—and that church will grow!

So do try it. Play down your titles and rules. Ease up on your membership requirements. You see, to us Woodstock kids, formal membership can feel like an unnecessary step backwards—maybe even a sellout to formality. Just meet our genuine needs in a genuinely celebrative environment, and we baby boomers might sign up—eventually.

Remember, *we boomers are searching for informality with meaning*. If and when we find it, we'll hang around with you long before our names appear on the church roster. We want to celebrate first. Will you allow that to happen?

Stress Relationships

Searching for informality with meaning translates that finding a church home where the congregation is cemented together through relationships rather than through creeds or doctrinal statements. In such a church, not only are formality and membership out, but casualness, participation and—yes—relationships are in.

In a recent worship service, one of our staff members suggested we all join hands and lift them to the sky, declaring that this was our position in the Body of Christ—a people whose hands and hearts have been joined, lifted and directed to Him as our resource, our point of adoration.

We've all touched one another in reaching out to Christ. So we all knew what that group action meant; it symbolized relationships—to Christ and to one another—that were high touch. Relationships within the Church should have been like that all along—at least, if you're a baby boomer, you probably believe that.

Building a relational community within the individual church means denominations will need to grow comfortable with a diversity of approaches. They will need to become astute at training leaders for small-group meetings and at coordinating a worship service that contains content and recognizable liturgy, yet is high in the human touch.

Worship settings must be casual yet substantive enough to reach the human heart. The listening grid of boomers won't allow them to hear a message that may be perfectly and purely presented, unless it embraces a style that is relevant to them. And that style will be built on relationships.

Boomers in the future then will flock to those churches in those denominations that are held together by the glue of relationships. This is not to say that orthodoxy and sound agreement on doctrinal statements aren't important, but the real adhesive strength of a church will lie in relationships.

Recognizing this fact will put pressure on all of us as we figure out how to keep our content intact. And the need to keep content intact will, in turn, require creative efforts on our part in presenting the creed and doctrinal statements that are essential to the purity of the Faith.

My concern, meanwhile, is that baby boomer peers will choose congregations still caught up in the proper, traditional structures and patterns of church life, only to be turned off by their formality, and then will become vulnerable to the often more efficient marketing and recruiting of cults and sects.

LOYALTY MUST BE WON

A vital question is: How can churches be informal, yet survive? In the 1990s and on into the next century, we will have to face the fact that institutions of all types will be viewed with suspicion. The Watergate mess in President Nixon's administration, the Iran-Contra blunder during Rea-

---

Boomers, in surprising numbers, are returning to church. And when they come, they bring with them specific needs. Understanding why these boomers have decided to return and what their needs are will help you and your church to serve them better.

---

gan's presidency, the scheming Ivan Boeskys of the world of high finance and, of course, the PTL and Jimmy Swaggart ministry scandals have made large institutions a suspicious commodity in our present culture.

Consequently, for my generation, loyalty to the church as an institution is out. Church loyalty for older church attenders is understood. However, church shopping and hopping are not perceived as poor practices in our baby boomer minds.

Nor do we give two hoots about your denominations.

We boomers are quite likely, in our lifetime, to become Baptist, Pentecostal, even Roman Catholic—or possibly all of the above at one time. And we will see very little incongruity with such a haphazard pilgrimage.

Lyle Schaller reports in his book, *It's a Different World!*, that, in 1965, 80 percent of the Methodist Church members said they had always been Methodists; 85 percent of the Baptists declared they'd always been Baptists; 75 percent of all Lutherans had always been Lutherans; 90 percent of the Catholics had always been Catholics; 66 percent of the Presbyterians reported that they had always been Presbyterians; and 60 percent of the Episcopalians had always been of that faith. Schaller further points out that those days are now long gone. Today, only a small percentage would consider themselves permanently affiliated with any particular group or denomination.[1]

With my age group you're only as good as your answer to this question: But what have you done for me lately? Our loyalty is only as deep as our local relationships are. After all, in the boomer's mind, excessive loyalty to any institution will only get you in trouble. Remember Watergate!

All this means then that churches will be successful in each community on the merits of each church alone. Any congregation then of any name or style that figures out how to break down formality and bring in genuine human touch will be effective in reaching my boomer age-group.

And the denominations which will thrive in the 1990s will be those who put their energies into making strong, local congregations and celebrate in the distinctive identities that each congregation will have in given cities. Encourage it; don't be frightened by varieties of style. How we understand church life in the future may require some radical redefinitions.

Why Boomers Are Returning to Church

> In the 1970s only 33.5 percent of baby boomers, born between 1946 and 1958, attended religious institutions, but 42.8 percent of the same group are attending now. Why are vanguard boomers, who skipped church in their 20s, returning in their 40s?[2]

Boomers, in surprising numbers, are returning to church. And when they come, they bring with them specific felt needs. Understanding why these boomers have decided to return and what their needs are will help you and your church to serve them better. Let's look at some of those needs.

• *Depression.* Depression is symptomatic of unmet expectations. Many boomers are facing a depressive view of life. Why? Because, as boomers, they are earning less than their folks did at every stage in life. Their expectations are not being met materially, which has led them to feel hemmed in, limited.

So they are seeking God out, hoping that He will help them move beyond those limitations. Perhaps they are imprisoned only by limitations on the exterior, but finding peace and freedom in the inner realm would also help them find release from external concerns. They hope, therefore, to be lifted out of the doldrums by our worship environment.

• *Family Values.* In a very real sense, boomers do have values, but aren't often aware of them. Now that boomers are having children of their own in growing numbers, they're looking for help to establish values that will make life sensible to their children.

They need churches to help them teach their kids morals and values, because they frankly don't know how. As they've rejected the values of their parents and society for so long, they are at a loss to know how to communicate them to their own children. They hope that our congregations can and will help in these areas.

• *New Age Burnout.* Boomers aren't afraid of any new stuff. They've experimented with a number of new religions, leaning toward the Far Eastern side. Boomers have read Shirley MacLaine's books and have gone *Out on a Limb* with her, but the majority aren't willing to do this anymore.

Now, they're turning to traditional outlets for their faith. Because they hope your congregation will offer stability, so they won't be able to handle any of the traditional in-house church squabbles. After all, one of the reasons they are attracted to you is the hope that you will stabilize their lives.

• *Postcrash Conversions.* In the wake of the 1987 stock market crash on Black Monday (October 19), many boomers looked to God to explain their new hardships. An example: "Attendance of New York stockbrokers in Bible study groups swelled from 60 to well over 200 just after the crash."[3]

• *Social Activism.* Boomers still believe they can change the world, and they hope your congregation will be interested in finding outlets to help their lives make a difference. They desire to be leaders in both their community and in your congregation.

While speaking with a young woman in our congregation, she said: "I hate my job, Pastor! It's so capitalistic. Everybody in my office thinks of nothing but making money. Now, don't get me wrong, Pastor, I like to make money too. But I also want my life to make a greater difference than that. Do you have any ideas?"

Allow me to pose a question to you pastors and church leaders: Do *you* have any ideas or outlets for boomers in your congregation?

• *Companionship.* Because so many baby boomers are single, they are on a quest for companionship. Mid-life couples, who have been relocated several times because of their vocations, are likewise looking for friendship and families with whom to share their growth.

Divorced and never-married boomers have now tired of serial relationships, and the specter of venereal diseases has sent them to seek out monogamous relationships. They really hope your church will offer them relational insights as well as opportunities.

• *Life Is Boring.* Baby boomers are now looking for some organization that is fun to be part of. They hope that, somewhere, life still has some carbonation—effervescence, sparkle—for the pizzazz has disappeared from their lives as they move into mid-life. They hope also that your congregation will be able to stimulate in them a new creativity and awareness that will cause life to challenge them anew.

Can you help them? Will you be able to help them? Are you set up to help them?

These are some of the primary expectations and needs that have led boomers to your church doors. An awareness of these concerns and an understanding of what boomers are looking for and need will prepare you to receive them.

If you can address these needs in a way that boomers can understand what you're saying to them and will create an intelligible environment for them, you will gain many good, lasting friends who will not only feel served, but will become enthusiastic about and will participate wholeheartedly in the life of your church. And they will happily assist your church in moving strongly and resolutely into the next century.

REVIEW

Let's conclude with a review of some basic how-tos on replacing formalism with high-touch, participative church life:

• *Action vs. Position*. Emphasis should be placed on action; i.e., what leaders *do* rather than what their titles might signify. Titles that aren't action-loaded should be used only with positional authority.

• *Be Committed to Having Fun*. Celebrate Christ's life with joy and spontaneity. A celebrative church life that is fun-filled and helps us to grow is essential to attract boomers to your church for any period of time. Fun, after all, is where peoples' lives touch each other the most positively. Humor and casualness are not in any way irreligious. Expressions of joy give way not only to a meaningful relationship with Christ, but with each other as well.

• *Programming*. When preaching and teaching, tell stories that emphasize relationships. Church programming ought to be geared toward making large-size and medium-size churches appear small by motivating people into high-touch opportunities.

• *Congregational Folklore*. Remember, every congregation has a life all its own. Celebrate it. Establish the folklore of your own local congregation. Encourage dialogues about the beliefs, people and events that make your congregation unique and what it is. *Omit, for the most part, talking about what makes a denomination distinctive*. Baby boomers may not mind hearing about it from time to time, but, by and large, this group will not relate to it.

• *Expressing Faith.* Developing action opportunities to express faith is tough, for the vast majority of us boomers are too busy to become involved easily. Yet boomers are altruistic; we desire to make an impact on the world around us. So we will remain forever mobile if we can't find churches that will engage us in action-oriented tasks.

We at Eastside Church have not been all that successful ourselves in engaging and involving people in ministry, but we are growing in an awareness of how to do it. When we were a smaller church, we began developing what we call "volunteer inventory lists." That's when we learned just how much work would be involved in coordinating volunteers.

Our church also learned that when couples share an assignment, they're far more willing to be involved. Based on our experience then, I would advise church leaders to encourage husbands and wives to volunteer for the same task together.

Still, our task is ever before us on how to become more efficient and effective in implementing volunteers for ministry work. The average American today gives four hours a week to volunteer services, and the figure may be even higher in churches. If statistics stand true, it appears then that churches are about to become the greatest expression of altruism yet seen.

But above all, remember that knowing why people visit your church is as important as knowing that they are there. As we move into this next century, it will be important for churches to test the waters of our culture to determine what kinds of expectations generate a continued interest or lack of interest in what we call "worship."

The demographic makeup of the 1990s church will be significantly different than that of the 1980s church. The church of this decade will have more singles. In fact, in many churches, new members will not only be boomers, they will also be *single* boomers with their own entirely different set of needs and expectations.

Are we ready for them? If not, how can we be prepared? Let's consider that question next.

Notes
  1. Lyle Schaller, *It's a Different World* (Nashville, TN: Abingdon Press, 1987), p. 25.
  2. *Boomer Report* 1 (March 1990), p. 4.
  3. Ibid. Adapted and supplemented with author comments.

3
LOOK OUT! THE SINGLES ARE COMING!

"An unmarried man is concerned about the Lord's affairs—how he can please the Lord."
—1 Corinthians 7:32

"Married couples with children, in 1970, were 40% of all American households, but now they are only 28%."
—American Demographics[1]

"No man is an island."
—John Donne[2]

Discovering the Hidden Majority

Our Senior Pastoral Team makes a practice of doing rigorous self-analysis following each of our services. We have learned to be ruthless about these evaluations. We seek to examine what the growth pattern is at our worship services, how well our programs work and whether our facilities are meeting our current needs.

One of our recent post-service analyses revealed that we already had parking problems at our six-month-old facility. Our auditorium will seat 1,400 people, with fixed seating for 1,200. Yet, in one of our services, with only 1,000 people present, we had just 40 parking slots left open.

According to our calculations, we should already have a quarter more parking spaces than we can ever use to fill our building. But obviously we did not. We now had to ask ourselves some serious questions.

I turned to Lucky, our consultant on facility issues, and asked, "Did we miscount the parking spots when we built this facility?"

Lucky, looking mildly flustered, assured me, "I counted them multiple times, Doug. We were okay. We might want to review it, however."

From our files we dug up the parking analysis. We had determined initially that the ratio of 2.3 people per slot was more than adequate for our facility. But, now, after just six months in our new building, we already had problems.

Our architect, our Pastor of Daily Operations, a couple of leaders from our building committee and I all joined Lucky to discuss this issue. Lucky rapidly punched the numbers into his calculator. Our architect slid out to the edge of his chair, his elbows on the table, his chin cupped in his hands, nervously tapping his foot.

With one eye on Lucky, I commented on how well the services had gone that day, while thinking to myself: *How did we mess up this much?*

The clicking of the calculator keys finally stopped. Lucky glanced up, smiling, yet also looking perplexed. As he pushed his glasses back up onto the bridge of his nose, he announced, "We are now parking 1.3 people per spot. That's our problem."

Within a few minutes we had established the primary problem. I'm embarrassed that we initially perceived an apparent evidence of growth as a problem. But we *did* have a problem. Why? Because we had miscalculated how the demographics of our community would affect our church plant.

We had known already that, in our particular community and in nearby neighborhoods, singles then numbered nearly 56 percent of the population. But we had underestimated how that shift toward singleness in our population would impact all the facilities of our church.

We glanced around the room at each other as I spoke: "You know, statistics showed us the number of singles in our area. And we prepared our staff, programming and so on accordingly, but we never considered the impact of singles on our parking needs. It is obvious that ministering to a large number of singles will require more parking spots."

Woodie, with his usual calm, commented: "Well, it's a reality we'll have to live with. I guess we'll just have to become the best church at reaching singles that has ever existed."

"I guess we'd better get more parking spots; otherwise, we'll miss out on half the people," LeRoy added.

Our architect then interjected: "I'm sure glad we discovered this before we constructed our next addition."

The outcome of our discussion was our realization that, to build the addition we had on the drawings before us, we needed to purchase a great deal more land than we had originally anticipated.

THE SINGLING OF THE CHURCH

Recently, demographers have confirmed that, possibly as early as 1991, the singles population in the United States will be in excess of 50 percent of all adults above the age of 18. Such figures mean we are faced with the "singling" of our communities.

This phenomenon is a new reality for the 1990s. Couples with children will no longer dominate our pews. Neither will married people represent a majority of the demographics in any church.

No one can say for certain what has caused this trend. Obviously, there are multiple factors. People are marrying later, and many more parents are single today. Too, many formerly married seniors are now single through bereavement. Our own congregation reflects very well the demographics of this shift to singleness.

This boomer generation is such a large one, that any statistical slant will have large ramifications for those seeking to serve them—and that means taking note of such trends as the increase in singles. For the larger proportion of singles in our society today is, in fact, a subgroup of the boomer generation.

And the singles population in America will impact the function of the Church in far more ways than just parking. When we in the church undertake programming, staffing, preaching, sharing illustrations or anecdotes and addressing needs from the pulpit, we had better keep in mind that half of our church population is single.

We also need to keep in mind the fact that singleness is a very complex and difficult issue, because it represents numerous age categories and life situations: teenagers who have moved out of their parents' homes, single moms in their late 20s, divorcees in their 40s with children, a growing number of single fathers, and the never marrieds of various ages, as well as the elderly—both widows and widowers.

This new reality of singleness is forcing the Church to face new issues when planning outreach and ministry. Consequently, when we discuss the issues of singles, we have to consider much more than just a one-lump segment of our population. Why? Because each age-group and life situation copes with quite different concerns and challenges. Consequently, each one requires different settings of fellowship, different ministry needs.

THE CHURCH BIAS AGAINST SINGLES

By and large though, the Church isn't ready for this aspect of the baby boomer's world, because the Church entertains biases against singles. These biases within the Christian community have prevented us from integrating and involving single people in the life and ministry of the Church. For far too long, singles have been relegated to special meetings somewhere in the basements of churches.

And, for just as long, singles have been unfairly and unkindly treated as a kind of oddity—persons that others have to tolerate and deal with until they finally get married. This attitude is the result of a basic disposition in the Church that if you're not married, you're either out of the will of God or your true love is still on the way to rescue you.

I can't remember how many times I've sat through unkind messages where not-so-subtle jabs were made at single people. The aim was to make them feel that when they were married, they would finally be happy—just as God intended them to be.

Singles aren't buying this kind of talk anymore. Given the fact that people, for the most part, are extremely intelligent, any single can look around and see that the 50 percent divorce rate is an undeniable indication that ultimate fulfillment is not found exclusively in a marital relationship. "Single and happy" may well be the battle cry of a large portion of the Church.

Stereotypically, too, singles are often thought of as being lounge lizards or swingers. This attitude is unfortunate for the simple reason that single people do have trouble with the whole issue of sexuality and, because they do, they are regarded as living "loose" lives. But anyone who has pastored for any length of time knows that this is a myth—a myth that needs to be destroyed. Married people struggle with their sexuality just as much as, if not more than, singles.

Obviously a great deal more respect needs to be given to singles in church life than has been true in the past. For continuing our negative attitudes will keep us from reaching a large segment of the boomer population—a generation with the highest percentage of singles in the history of mankind.

Congregations across the country will have to face these biases squarely and correct them, for stereotypical thinking won't fly in the 1990s. Instead, serious thought needs to be given as to how to include and involve singles in very visible expressions of church life and leadership. Otherwise single people will continue to feel slighted by the Church, and they will go on shunning the Church that shuns them.

How did the Church in America come by these unfortunate attitudes toward singles? For understanding, let's return to yesteryear, to pre-"Leave It to Beaver" times. We'll find at least part of our answer there.

In 1944, 2.3 million marriages took place—29 percent more than in the previous year. The next year, 2 million marriages occurred and, in 1949, 1.8 million marriages took place.[3] During this heyday of marriage, public opinion turned against the unmarried. By the mid-1950s, more than half the American public believed that people who did not want to marry were either "sick" or abnormally selfish.

What the Church today often characterizes as a "return to traditional values" really means those values of the late 1940s and early 1950s. Yet these years of nearly universal marriage are actually unique and untraditional in American history. For at the turn of this century most young women were *un*married.

Cornell University professor, Edward L. Kain, recently stated: "Young Americans are returning to levels of singlehood that have been characteristic throughout the history of this country—but which were interrupted by a few decades of unusually high marriage rates and low ages at the onset of marriage."[4]

Cheryl Russell, writing for *American Demographics* magazine, has stated also: "In 1985, 59% of women in their early twenties were single, up from 36% in 1970. One-fourth of women in their late twenties have never married, up from 11% in 1970. Women in their early thirties are twice as likely to be single today as women in that age group in 1970."[5]

In contrast, women my mother's age were married in astonishing numbers. By 1950, only 32 percent of the women, age 20 to 24, were unmarried. During the post-war years in the 1940s, many women married before the age of 20.[6]

What the Church needs to realize is that this high rate of marriage, and at earlier ages, is unique to the decade of the consumer generation's development. The present state of singleness is not all that peculiar in a larger historical perspective.

Singleness, in other words, is really quite a normal phenomenon and not an evident aberration of the baby boom generation. Predictably, some of the stronger churches in America in the next decade will, in fact, be pastored by single men and women!

THE BIBLE AND SINGLENESS

The apostle Paul argues in 1 Corinthians 7 that it is preferable for a believer to be single, because a single person is afforded greater opportunities to serve God and to further His gospel. A careful reading of Paul's words in this chapter leaves no doubt that, by comparison, the marital state was less desirable.

And since Paul felt that a single person could more easily be "concerned about the Lord's affairs—how he can please the Lord" (v. 32), he plainly encouraged the Church to remain single. The apostle's counsel contrasts sharply with generally held views in church life today. Yet, in the age of the baby boomer, Paul's position makes a great deal of sense.

Now, I'm not suggesting or advocating that we stand up on a Sunday morning and discourage our single people from marrying. But I am suggesting that this Scripture allows us plenty of room to rechannel the gospel so that it is not being oriented only toward the "traditional American family." Perhaps we have associated the gospel too closely with "family" life, rather than placing its emphasis upon our becoming happy, fulfilled individuals in Christ, which, in turn, could help our marital relationships.

After all, marriage is not the ultimate fulfillment of humanity; Jesus Christ is. And Jesus Himself was never married, nor was the apostle Paul, nor the great pastor, Timo-

---

Much of our talk about the nuclear family may...be the reflection of a 1950s culture that is long gone. And our invoking the past as though it were still the present makes us unintelligible...in today's culture.

---

thy. Of those in the early apostolic leadership of the Church, only the family of Peter is mentioned. Though volumes are written in the New Testament on other subjects, only a few minor instructions are given to Christians about the marriage relationship.

Nevertheless, our Church today is still as patriarchal as was our culture of the 1950s. The United States was intoxicated by its great victories. Some sort of sociological testosterone flowed through our society. After all, we had survived two world wars and the Great Depression, and now it was time to conquer our own land.

Much of our talk about the nuclear family and the strong

patriarchal orientation of our congregations may not be as biblically sound as we have thought. Rather, they may, in fact, be the reflection of a 1950s culture that is long gone. And our invoking the past as though it were still the present makes us unintelligible to that hidden majority of singles in today's culture.

So integrating boomer singles in your congregation will require more than simply accepting them. It will also require understanding—and presenting—the positive side of being a Christian single as well.

I have found singles to be a great blessing to our congregation. And I'm glad that there is little notice or discussion in our congregation or in our leadership about who is single and who is married. Admittedly, however, it has taken a great deal of work to reach this point.

MINISTERING TO SINGLES

With our society over half single, shouldn't this statistical fact alone cause us to adjust our thinking and reevaluate the illustrations we use in sermons, the disbursement of funds to various church programs and the makeup of our church leadership? I think so. And there are practical steps the Church can take to make baby boomers feel included. Here are some:

Collect Accurate Data

Each year at Eastside Church we have a session in which we try to plan ahead at least two years. Initially, several of us from our senior staff met, then we broadened the discussion to include the entire staff.

In 1987, we purchased some recent demographic data on our immediate neighborhood. Then Mike, my assistant pastor; Lucky, our Pastor of Daily Operations; and I sat down at our conference table with charts, diagrams and statistics spread out from one end to the other.

Our services had been filled to capacity for a number of months. We were running four services on Sundays, with church attendance now exceeding 2,300 in a building that comfortably seated only 500! We were bone-tired and needed fresh insight on how to continue reaching our immediate community.

As I flipped through the census materials for our area, I noticed an interesting figure. I held it up to examine it more closely and said to Mike, "Get this. There are 10,000 single mothers within three miles of our church!"

Lucky interjected, "That explains why our counseling load is so disproportionate with single mothers. I thought we were just an extremely compassionate group—or that there were a lot of shiftless husbands in our neighborhood."

Mike, who understood the meaning of this figure far better than Lucky or I did and who headed several College/Career Single outreach groups and once-a-month meetings, jumped in. "I don't have any trouble believing that at all. I know that whenever we have a special event of our College/Career Singles Group, there's usually a need for child care."

"Well, how many singles are there in our neighborhood?" I asked.

As we thumbed through the various papers, we found that, because our area has a large number of apartments, it contains an extremely high percentage of single people.

I glanced over at Mike as he leaned back in his chair, cupping his hands behind his head. "What do you think, Mike?"

He responded: "I think it's an unusual day to be ministering. I think I've got a great idea to relieve our pressure on Sunday mornings and reach some of these single people as well. What if we started a Friday night service, just for single people—you know, from college age up to about 30 years old?"

Learn about and speak to the felt needs of singles in our congregations. Just as marrieds have needs, so do single people have needs that should be addressed...in the context of the Church.

Right then, Lucky leaned over the table, flipped through his stack of research and asked somewhat anxiously, "Every week? You mean Mike will do an event every week?"

I now got back into the conversation. "No, Lucky. We'll have a regular service for single people, and we'll advertise it as a service just for single people. The data confirm that there's a need for this.

"A Friday night service will relieve the crunch on Sunday mornings, and will also provide an opportunity for this age-group to gather together. But let's make certain we watch and analyze the data closely to see if our congregation is proportionately represented in our community."

After this meeting with the senior staff, we decided to go for it. We then began the Friday night service and, within six months, well over 200 singles were attending, with an aggregate of 800 people. This service, called the "College/ Career Singles Service," continues to grow to this day.

We then discovered the need for two singles services and fellowships: one for those 30 and older, and one for those 35 and younger. We've also found it necessary to have parenting classes for single mothers.

Dispel the Myths

The stereotypical view of singles being neurotically lonely, incredibly homely and sociologically retarded pervades churches. These myths must go! Let's embark on a campaign to make sure all stereotypical biases disappear from our churches.

Present Singles in a Positive Light

Presenting singles in a very positive light is essential. I recently had the privilege of sitting in on a private lecture given by Dr. John R. W. Stott, an Anglican priest who is rector of All Souls Church, London, and honorary chaplain to Queen Elizabeth II of England. Early on, Dr. Stott—who has enjoyed a long and distinguished ministry—felt God's call to celibacy. It would be well to have models like Dr. Stott speak to our congregations—models who can remove the negative biases regarding singleness.

Address Felt Needs of Singles

Learn about and speak to the felt needs of singles in our congregations. Just as marrieds have needs, so do single people have needs that should be addressed. But the needs of single people are more likely to go unmet if not given some attention in the context of the Church.

Some of these needs are:

- Companionship
- Support

- Reassurance
- Warmth and affection
- Confrontation
- Self-understanding
- Freedom from past harmful situations.[7]

There is no better place for single persons to be welcomed and have their needs met and addressed than in a local church. I would advise you pastors to meet with groups of singles regularly to ask them to share their felt needs so that you can address them in your sermon messages.

I've been teaching our College Career Singles at the Friday night services on a regular basis. Following one week's service, I sat down with 20 of this group's leaders and asked them to tell me what topics they felt I talked too much about, as well as what topics they wished I would cover in the future. I walked away with a list of about 40 issues, several of which would never have occurred to me had I not met with them first.

Since I married at the age of 20 myself, I have little experience as a single. So I needed that input from the singles on the topics I would be teaching them on Friday nights. Having that input, I believe, has increased my effectiveness in reaching a large section of our congregation whom I love and serve.

Evaluate Communication Styles

If we pastors use illustrations that relate only to the nuclear family, we can alienate single persons without realizing it. We must make deliberate efforts to include examples and anecdotes that deal with the single person's world.

And we need to rethink comments about divorce. If 50 percent of all marriages are ending in divorce, a significant number of divorcées are likely to be in our congregations, among them perhaps even single mothers experiencing the agony of a recent divorce.

Besides gathering a list of needs from singles, I've tried to become single in my imagination as I prepare my Sunday messages. In your imagination, visit your own congregation as a single mother. This exercise can help you develop greater sensitivity towards this segment of the boomer population in your church.

Ruthless self-analysis of our preaching and teaching is essential if we are going to develop the sensitivity necessary in our messages for communicating the gospel effectively to boomer singles.

Provide Gathering Opportunities

Besides determining and addressing the felt needs of singles, it is essential to provide them with opportunities for worship and fellowship. In the past, because singles were considered a small minority, many churches that could have had strong singles groups assumed erroneously that there were too few singles in their fellowship to form such a group. Yet every congregation of several hundred people will have a significant number of single adults, allowing for several kinds of groups to be started.

In 1988, we started our first singles group, the College Career Singles, and began meeting every Friday night. We call this service the "College Career Singles Service" and run it as though it were any other worship service.

Within a matter of months, our singles group had grown by 200 to 300 people, with an aggregate of 800 involved. I was surprised by the response until I seriously evaluated the number of singles in our church-at-large. As a result of this evaluation, we have evolved into at least four different kinds of singles groups, all in different stages of development in our congregation.

So I would encourage conscientious church leaders to consider at least four different groups themselves, as follows:

1. One group would be for those in their 20s to mid-30s.
2. A second group would consist of those singles, ages 35 and up. A large percentage of these individuals will have been divorced and will need special classes on surviving divorce. This group will also require opportunities for significant social gatherings.
3. A third group would minister to divorcées with children or to single mothers who have never been married. This group will need to be singled out because of their special needs. It's difficult enough to be the mother of and caring for a toddler, let alone also supporting the family. The Church can be of incredible service to these young women.
4. A fourth group would minister to widows and widowers. Several decades, on average, separate this group from the others.

If your congregation is not large enough to start your own singles meetings, I would suggest networking with other groups of singles. Usually, if a church doesn't number 2,000 to 3,000, it feels somewhat inhibited about caring for singles. However, many great groups are already gathering in most cities. Even announcing events for single people that are being held elsewhere under other auspices is an important way to communicate that you desire to serve and help singles as well as families.

Involve Singles in Leadership

Involving singles in leadership is another important step for every congregation which desires to reach out to baby boomers. Often, for that matter, single people can lead with greater devotion and intensity than married people.

I believe firmly that the makeup of gifted leadership in a congregation will precede the ministry that happens. For this reason I deliberately encourage and recruit single people to be in viable leadership positions in our church. So several years ago, when I became concerned about the lack of single involvement in leadership, I met with the nominating committee of our church council and asked them to consider seriously nominating several single people of varying ages to be voted on by our congregation for leadership positions.

When our ministry team met recently to discuss this topic, we were stunned by the bias we had against single people. How is it that we so easily overlook the single person when looking for leadership in the Church? A partial answer may lie in the fact that the greater portion of our ministry staff is married, so we tend to focus on people like ourselves, forgetting about the single segment of our church population.

We realized that our staff also needed to include single people who express ministry. So we've made certain that we have the representation of single people on our council. And in other categories of church leadership, such as volunteer pastors and ministry team members, we've also deliberately included single people. It is exciting to see what happens as we take steps in this direction. For any efforts to include single persons in the core life of the church is greatly appreciated by them, as well as being very fruitful in its impact on them and the church.

Yet making certain that we give an adequate platform to single people in our congregation does take conscious effort. Knowing this to be true, churches of the 1990s need to commence now involving and equipping single persons for significant leadership roles. Only then will we be intelligible to the boomer generation and able to express a gospel of sensitivity to boomer singles.

Attitudes of Church Leaders

Church leaders particularly need to work on and change their attitudes towards single persons and boomers. Take the following viewpoints seriously and share them with other church leaders. These directives can serve to guide us in our approach to single boomers as we seek to minister to them and to their particular needs:

1. Understand that singleness is a recognized phenomenon.
2. Emphasize singleness as an accepted status in the life of the Church.
3. Encourage and celebrate single ministers.
4. Give attention to the health, care and strengthening of single mothers.
5. Present marriage in a more balanced and realistic perspective.

Christianity is for all humanity, whatever our situations may be—whether we are married or single. Hopefully, the Church will find the balance needed to minister effectively to this boomer generation.

WHAT NEXT?

The Barna Research Group of Glendale, California, has found many reasons why singles do not attend church. According to George Barna's research, the most common reasons for not attending church were problems of time and priority. Most singles said they had to work on Sunday or that it was their only day off. They also said that other issues in their lives took precedence over church attendance. Barna further reported that the typical all-American single stated that she or he also needed Sunday for doing other activities to keep life and limb together.[8]

These statistical insights make a good case for having special services at times more appropriate for singles. It may sound prejudicial—and probably is—but perhaps there is some truth in the statement that singles tend to get more obscure working hours.

Only 30 percent of the singles tested by the Barna Research Group had a negative disposition toward church attendance as such, while another 30 percent were undecided.[9]

Almost four out of 10—or 39 percent—unchurched singles said they had a positive disposition toward attending church in the future.[10,11] This finding means that at least four out of every 10 single people in our communities would be happy to attend our churches *if we will reach out to them in a friendly, accommodating manner.* Will we?

Hopefully, your imagination is allowing a boomer church to begin taking shape in your mind, a church which will be relationship-friendly and single-sensitive. For, as we have seen, a boomer church has to be casual, informal, high on relationships and one with a significant number of single people in its fellowship.

Another practical step to take in developing churches that baby boomers will repeatedly visit and become part of is *a step towards the pragmatic gospel.* If you haven't walked through the how-to section of your bookstore lately, do so before you read the next chapter. In this section of a bookstore you will find the vital key for communicating to boomers in a way they will appreciate and look forward to when returning to their pews in your church.

Notes

1. "The New Demographic Reality of Families," *American Demographics* (June 1989) quoted in "Average U.S. Citizen: Married Woman 32," *USA Today,* May 15, 1989, p. 3-A.
2. John Donne, *Devotions upon Emergent Occasions* (1624), no. 17.
3. Cheryl Russell, *One Hundred Predictions for the Baby Boom* (New York: Plenum Press, 1987), p. 29.
4. Russell, *op. cit.,* p. 87.
5. Ibid.
6. Russell, *op. cit.,* p. 30.
7. William Lyon, *A Pew for One, Please: The Church and the Single Person* (New York: Crossroads Books, Seabury Press, 1977), p. 107. A synopsis of entire chapter.
8. Barna Research Group, *Single Adults in America* (Glendale, CA: Barna Research Group, 1987), pp. 3-11.
9. Barna Research Group, *op. cit.,* p. 20.
10. Ibid.
11. The entirety of this research would be helpful to anyone seeking an intelligent outreach to single baby boomers. To obtain *Single Adults in America,* write: Barna Research Group, 722 West Broadway, Glendale, CA 91204.

4

HAVE YOU WALKED THROUGH THE HOW-TO SECTION LATELY?

"I believe in God, but why go to church?"
—30-year-old in my office

Do you own a VCR that still flashes 12:00? If so, you haven't learned how to operate your video recorder yet. But don't feel bad. I haven't learned how to set my VCR on "record" either.

As I operate my Macintosh computer, I can glance across the room, over a stack of books, and see the little red light flashing 12:00. And it really aggravates me. The manual tells me it's easy. But I've tried, and I just can't seem to figure the thing out.

SIMPLIFY THE MANUAL

A friend's advice was simply, "Read the manual again."

I *have* read that crazy manual a dozen times. The language is too specialized for a layman like me to understand. I've concluded that the problem with it—and with many other manuals—is that the guy who invented the machine also wrote the manual.

I heard on the "Oprah Winfrey Show" the other day that you can hire guys to guide you through the operation of your home machinery, such as VCRs. These guys are the modern equivalent of the last century's wilderness guides.

I think unchurched people often feel about church the way I do about my VCR. Church just doesn't seem to be "user friendly." And the would-be guides are too accustomed to church life to make church intelligible to baby boomers.

Church will have to become very user friendly to attract boomers. We don't have the patience to work through too much unclarity. We're good spectators; then we want to participate, so make it easy for us.

I remember attending church for the first time when I was 18. I found it horrifying! Then I had a dynamic

---

Preach very practical messages to us: down-to-earth, how-to messages that tell boomers this God-stuff is real and is meant for everyday life.

---

encounter with Christ. But even then, understanding this church stuff was rugged. These church people took so many things for granted that didn't make the slightest bit of sense to me.

My first offering experience shook me up, because I didn't know how much to give. And the collection bags looked really odd to me. In addition, I could sing hardly any of the songs because I didn't know them. Yet everyone else—except for a couple of other social outcasts like me—knew.

Because my first introduction to the church world was so traumatic, I have determined to make it easier for other people like me to return to and enjoy church life.

WHAT GOD DO WE PREACH?

The boomers' problem with God has never been whether He is real or not. We just wonder if He is important. So if you really believe Christ is important, then tell us how and

in what ways He is important. Convince us that you celebrate a God who is involved in the lives of His people
Monday through Friday. Do that, and we'll keep coming
back for more.

Remember, we boomers don't come to church because
doing so is the accepted gesture to make. We come to *get!*
We expect to get something that we can use—messages
that apply to our lives.

Being a boomer myself, I understand what boomers
hope to get when they came to church. Often as I look out
across the faces of the congregation I serve each week, I
pray that God will help me to show them He is important
to each one of them and that He won't sleep in on Monday
mornings. That's why I make a practical life-application the
highlight of each of my messages.

And along with presenting practical, life-related messages, we at Eastside Church strive to maintain a caring
environment that is characterized by love, acceptance and
forgiveness. For reaching the unchurched boomer, this com-
bination of practicality and loving concern is unbeatable.

So, remember, one of the best ways you can demonstrate the importance of God to boomers is to give us messages that apply to our daily lives. Preach very practical
messages to us: down-to-earth, how-to messages that tell us
this God-stuff is real and is meant for everyday life. We like
that; that appeals to us because it touches us where we live.

We are interested in a God who is vitally interested in
and concerned about our daily lives. For inwardly, we think
such thoughts as: *There may be eternal life, but right now,
Monday through Friday is enough eternity for me.* Have
Christ and Church make sense to our world, and we'll be
back. Until then, forget it!

Why do we think such thoughts? In part perhaps,
because our American culture suffers from a terribly inade-

quate view of God. A favorite film of mine that illustrates one cultural distortion of God is a movie entitled, *Time Bandits*, produced by ex-Beatle, George Harrison, and his film company.

This movie is about a group of young boys and dwarfs who steal the map of time and space from God. God periodically searches for the bandits, asking for the map's return. In the final scene of the movie, when God catches up with the little thieves, He appears as a harmless, tottering old fool. The actor who played God portrayed Him as someone who could probably do most anything if He put forth the effort. But, in this film, God seemed to be only half-hearted about everything.

This half-hearted effort on God's part created great pressure on the time bandits, for they had expected more—much more. I wonder if Harrison and his writers plugged into the psyche of the baby boomer generation. For one of our great fears about God is that He may turn out to be only half-hearted about this whole scenario depicting Christ and His Church. Our lives are too important to us to be entrusted to a half-hearted God.

That's why we want to be shown and experience a whole-hearted God—the dynamic God of the Bible! One of the ways you can show us this God is to bring His Word into our lives and homes.

One of my favorite books is *Your God Is Too Small* by J. B. Phillips. In this powerful book, Phillips calls on Christians to rid ourselves of false idols. He defines an idol as "a wrong view of God." Idols that portray God as the angry policeman in heaven must be dispelled and destroyed. Nor is the innocuous Santa Claus figure to be tolerated.

Show us how God in Christ, as Hebrew 4:15 affirms, faced sexual temptation, the specter of addiction or the challenge to be truthful and yet remained holy and honest.

Let us know that our God is aware of the pressures of parenting or of the ups-and-downs of the life of a salesman, and we'll be back and bring our friends as well.

Imagine with me, if you will, the following scenario:

For illustrative purposes, let's create a family and call them Bob and Betty Boomernosky. They are in their late 30s and live in middle-class suburban America. The time is 7:45 A.M. on a Sunday morning.

The alarm has just rung. Reaching over to turn it off, Bob moans and asks Betty, "Why did you set the clock this early today? It's Sunday."

Betty, rubbing her eyes, tries to remember. Ah-ha, it comes to her. "Oh, now I remember. Randy and Ruth Boomerson asked us to go to church with them today. The kids are really looking forward to it."

Betty leans back on one elbow as she waits for Bob's response.

"Oh, yeah, I forgot." Bob slowly acknowledges their commitment. Then he rolls over and tries to sleep some more.

Five minutes later, Betty chides Bob as she pokes him. "Come on, Bob! We can't let them down again."

With this masterful use of guilt, Betty gets Bob out of bed and on his feet.

As he cleans up and gets ready, he asks, "Is this going to be boring? I mean, Randy seems like a nice-enough guy and all, but I don't think I can take any guilt trips or boring stuff."

Betty walks over to the phone and calls Ruth. "Hi, Ruth. I just wanted to let you know that we're about ready to go with you. We should probably just follow you."

"Oh, Ruth, what will your pastor be talking about today?" she asks, hopeful that it will be something to ease Bob's reluctance.

As Betty strolls back into the bathroom, she looks enthused and says, "Bob, Ruth says their pastor will be talking about 'Three Ways to Keep Your Energy up During the Week While on the Job.'"

"From the Bible?" Bob asks skeptically.

"I don't know. I suppose so. It sounds interesting anyway, doesn't it?"

Together the family strolls out the door to their car.

Okay, maybe there isn't really anyone named Boomerson or Boomernosky. But the scenario isn't all that far removed from reality.

THE SELF-HELP GENERATION

Several years ago we conducted an unscientific survey in our church. We asked people how they came to be fellowshiping at Eastside Foursquare Church. Nearly nine out of 10 said they had been brought by a friend or relative.

That's how most growing churches grow—one person at a time, one contact at a time. So, if you can get a few of us baby boomers satisfied with our church experience, we'll bring our friends back with us, just as Randy and Ruth Boomerson did.

Societal pressures bring few of us to church these days. And we really aren't interested in how accurate your church government is. Nor do we really care for your opinion on El Salvador or your interpretation of the theological significance of Romans 6-9. Instead, we want to know how to *do* Christianity. So *each Sunday, help us by giving us practical tools for everyday living in an intelligible message.*

We boomers have been called the "Pepsi Generation," the "Vietnam Generation," the "Woodstock Generation" and the "Spock Generation." And when it comes to choosing a church, we are also the "How-to Generation."

You see, we thirty somethings are suspicious of experts. We believe we can do it just as well ourselves if you give us the right tools. This attitude may explain the success of the how-to section of most bookstores. We've all seen them— self-help books that tell us how to do everything from *How to Love Your Job* to *How to Train Your Dog Yourself in Ten Easy Steps*. I even came across this title recently: *How to Be a Guilty Parent.*

I recommend this helpful exercise to all church leaders, whether you're a lay leader or a professional. Load up your church board in a car after your next meeting and head for B Dalton Bookseller or Crown Books. Once you arrive, go straight to the self-help section. See if each of you can come up with three ideas for a practical sermon from the titles in this section.

Periodically, I actually conduct this very exercise with my own church board. And it's always a refreshing experience to realize that people really are searching for God, and that the gospel addresses all areas of human needs.

People respond positively when they see your topics are taking their life challenges seriously. This is why we aim practical topics at our women's studies, men's studies and home groups. We want our people to know the *one-and-only God who is alive and of the living!*

WHAT'S THE TAKE-AWAY?

We've already noticed that practical sermon titles will attract boomers to a particular church. But getting their attention and holding it is not the same thing. So when we preach, we have to deliver—and deliver quickly.

It used to be a lot simpler in times past to get peoples' attention. The margin of error was really quite large. But today, people have televisions with four-foot screens in their living rooms. And, in the next room, they have stereos with better high fidelity quality than that of the studio equipment on which the Beatles recorded and produced "Sgt. Pepper's Lonely Hearts Club Band" 20 years ago.

So when I preach, I figure I have about one or two minutes for people to decide if they want to listen to me or not.

> *Your basic boomer is interested in the Bible, but you have to get us over the fear of getting lost in Genesis 1 and 2. As we're the most educated generation in history, we aren't lacking in intelligence. Rather, our fear is that we will look stupid.*

It's for this reason that I like to state my "take away" points up front.

And what's a take-away, you ask? It is what I can expect a listener to take away from my message—those message points that will walk out the door with him or her.

Let me illustrate. Let's say I'm going to teach from the third chapter of John about being born again. Now, I'm not going to tell my congregation that I'm going to explain the process of regeneration to them.

No, instead I would say something like, "Today we're going to see what Jesus has to say about starting all over again. Have any of you wished you could start life all over? Listen closely and we'll learn how to do just that."

Voila! I've got their ear!

Publishers harp at authors all the time about take-aways. They say a buyer will ask such questions as: What is this book about for which I'm about to overpay you? Does it have something applicable to my life?

Imagine now that our listeners sitting in our pews are thinking, while opening their Bibles to that day's text: *Will the pastor say anything that's important for me today?*

SERMON SUGGESTIONS THAT ATTRACT BABY BOOMERS

Your basic boomer is interested in the Bible, but you have to get us over the fear of getting lost in Genesis 1 and 2. As we're the most educated generation in history, we aren't lacking in intelligence. Rather, our fear is that we will *look* stupid.

So, you can begin by assuming that we are already interested in the Bible. Just show us some enthusiasm for the Bible in your own life and we will be affected. For starters, here are a few, practical ideas:

1. Visit those how-to sections in your local bookstores.
2. Regularly have a small group submit a list of their greatest challenges at home and on the job.
3. Similarly, acquire inventories of needs from several secular people in your community.
4. Periodically, examine issues of *Time, Newsweek* and *USA Today*, as these publications tend to be on the cutting edge of the felt needs and fears that people are facing.
5. Apply practical aims to every study, message or program in your church.

6. Practice composing practical, catchy titles for your messages (sermons) from various biblical texts.
7. Limit your preaching to roughly 20 minutes, because boomers don't have too much time to spare. And don't forget to keep your messages light and informal, liberally sprinkling them with humor and personal anecdotes.

It is very important for congregational leaders to gather needs inventories regularly, as felt needs are very fluid and in a general state of flux at any given time. A few years back, I preached frequently about children's needs. Now, mid-life issues often take center stage.

Taking my own advice, I regularly gather a group of people together and have them list the greatest issues (1) that they are currently facing, and (2) that they would like me to address. Recently I asked the question: What are your seven most pressing needs or fears you would like to have addressed in our Sunday messages?

The nine most-mentioned issues were:

1. How can I have a happier marriage?
2. How can I handle my money better?
3. I don't like my job. What can I do about it?
4. How do I get guidance about my employment?
5. Will I be caught in an ACOA (adult children of alcoholics) pattern all my life?
6. How did we get the Bible? How do I know it's God's Word?
7. How can I be a better parent?
8. How can I get more time for myself?
9. How can I feel better about myself?

I keep this list and other similar lists on file, study them regularly and select from them topics for Sunday messages. And always, I use the following yardstick: Am I addressing the areas of their challenges?

THE REWARDS ARE GREAT

Now don't misunderstand me; I'm not claiming to be the greatest practical preacher there is. In fact, public speaking has never come naturally to me. So preaching is a great deal of work for me.

I wish to share the following letter with you from a young woman in our congregation, and I hope it will encourage you church leaders to speak about the God who is important to us all in our everyday lives:

Dear Pastor Doug:

I wanted to stop and thank you for the practical way you bring the Scriptures to our lives every Sunday. When I was younger, I went to church with my parents. We never discussed the Bible much at home. We really never expected the worship experience to have anything to do with living from Monday to Friday.

After being gone from the Church for about 15 years, it has been a necessity to know that this Christian stuff relates and has something to do with Monday morning.

This Sunday I brought my friend Susan from work. I kept sharing with her. She came to our church to hear something real practical. I was concerned because you announced you were going to be doing the series on John. Sure enough, you

said two or three things that brought John right
into Monday for us.

My friend accepted Christ that Sunday, and
can't wait to come back with me this weekend.
Thanks. All our friends wish their pastors would
talk about the kind of things you do.

Sincerely,

Our church for baby boomers is gradually taking shape.
As you step into our foyer, you notice that the majority of
the adults are single. The atmosphere is very casual, warm,
easygoing and friendly. As you glance down at the bulletin
handed you, you note a very practical message on "How to
Start Life All Over." Someone shakes your hand and
promptly invites you to a home Bible study group.

If you're a boomer, you're thinking to yourself: *Hey,
I've never had it so good. I think I'll videotape Sunday's
football game every week so I don't miss out on what's happening here.*

But wait, what about the kids of boomers? How are they
affecting our journey back to God? Actually, the boomer
church is high on kids. And the kids of boomers have folks
who expect Grandma's kind of care and the squeaky clean
atmosphere of Disneyland for their kids! Read the next
chapter and find out why.

5

WHAT ABOUT GOD, DADDY?

*We thirty something people
are being awakened to the fact
that we have become the escorts for
another generation.*
—Doug Murren

SHARON was a single mom in her early 40s and had attended our church for several months. Now, following an evening service, she asked to speak with me.

"Pastor, I'd like to commit my life to Christ. I did once when I was a kid, but I want to again."

Sharon held back tears as she asked me to pray with her. We prayed briefly, and Sharon had a wonderful, redeeming experience.

Curious about how she had come to join our ranks, I asked? "How did you end up here at Eastside?"

"Actually, it was my kids. We'd tried a few places, but my kids really love your youth program here. Everything seemed geared to them. I came mainly because I felt guilty about Joe and our breakup. On my first visit, I was surprised by how much I enjoyed it."

WE NEED YOUR HELP WITH OUR CHILDREN

I have heard dozens of similar stories—all from parents who are looking for help. The social upheaval of the '60s has definitely gone to seed in the '80s and the '90s. And we thirty something people are being awakened to the fact that we have become the escorts for another generation. Our children are our prized possession, though family life hasn't gone all that well for us boomers.

Well over 50 percent of us have divorced and most have remarried. Our family lives are very complex. We are still searching and our concern for our kids has interjected itself right into the middle of all this marrying, divorcing and blending.

The parenting experience of my folks' generation could be characterized as paranoiac. By our very numbers we were really an unmanageable lot. The boomer population explosion taxed every school system to its limits. We drove classroom sizes to excess and our parents tried to manage a group of kids that outnumbered them almost two to one.

Children are a great motivation in causing parents to consider a church life for their family. When our children begin school, we often start thinking about their spiritual development as well.

I would characterize my own generation's parenting experience as guilt-ridden. We felt guilty about our divorces. We felt guilty about our life-styles. We failed to say no when we should have. And we said yes when we shouldn't have to drugs and all sorts of addictions and aberrations in large numbers.

We harvested the sad results of "If it feels good, do it." And now we feel quite guilty about all of it. The polls show that we boomers don't want our kids experimenting with sex and drugs the way we did.

So we boomer parents want to know if your churches are ready to invest in our kids. If we boomers are going to stick around, we are really going to need your help with our children. For our kids are asking us very tough ques-

tions for which we don't have the right answers—questions
about God, about sex, about matters we never thought
we'd have to think that much about.

THE CHURCH'S NEED TO RESPOND

As both pastor and parent myself, I have observed that children are a great motivation in causing parents to consider a
church life for their family. When our children begin
school, we often start thinking about their spiritual development as well. This fact is surprisingly true of baby boomer
parents who evaluate congregations by how much they
value children.

Admittedly, reaching out to and caring for kids is never
cost-effective, *though any church that genuinely invests in
kids will grow.* A baby boomer-oriented church, therefore,
will invest heavily in its youth budget—and the investment
will be well worth every cent spent.

Yet you can't care for kids from the sole standpoint of
having your church grow. So motive is a big issue here, for
churches must allow the Lord to develop an authentic love
of children in their hearts and programs.

As a pastor, however, I don't think the Church world, as
a whole, has taken this great need seriously. Adequately
staffing this department in our own church, for instance,
has been a constant struggle, because people really aren't
being trained for children's ministry or youth work.

Nevertheless, several years ago I was shown by the Holy
Spirit that, if we at Eastside Church were going to reach
baby boomers, we would need to prepare ourselves first,
so we could do a good job of helping to train their kids.
For some time, Eastside Church had to rent a facility. Even
then, however, we tried to develop a quality-conscious
environment for our kids.

In doing so, we were mindful that unchurched people give two reasons why they attend a particular church regularly:

- They are made to feel welcome, and
- The church has a strong youth program.

I remember going to Sunday School once in the fourth grade. I can't remember if I had been invited or if I just wanted to go one Sunday. My folks didn't attend church, so Mom dropped me off. For parents to drop their kids off at church, but not go themselves was a pretty common practice back then. I don't think this is likely to happen with boomers, however. If we send our kids to church, we're committed also.

Anyway, I remember walking into a dimly lit, uninviting room down in the dark basement of this church. Just a bit of light came from one small window about seven feet above the concrete floor. To a little fourth-grader, it seemed like 30 or 40 feet up to that window.

An empty chair in a circle of beat-up chairs awaited me when I entered the room. An old, worn-out rug that someone must have donated centered the cheerless and otherwise barren room. Mrs. Johnson, the teacher, acted as though she wasn't too thrilled to be there herself, that she was just putting in her time.

Of course, I didn't have a Bible. I didn't know anything about the Bible. But the rest of the kids had theirs, and it was obvious they knew the Bible well.

I was sure I was the only dummy there. I finished that morning with the combined experience of having been scared, uneasy, humiliated, bored and cold in that church basement. I never returned.

Boomers won't bring their kids into this kind of setting. They expect something better from our churches. Our sophisticated culture, including the high quality of television production, has elevated their standards of what is acceptable. Quality consciousness and present-day standards ensure that competition for the child's ear and the parents' trust is high in our society.

REVERSE EVANGELISM

One million more Americans turned 40 in 1986 than in 1985. Similarly, one million more turned 40 in 1984 than did so in 1983. These figures mean that large numbers of baby boomer parents now have teenagers living at home. And those same parents are looking to the Church for help.

I truly believe that the most cost-effective program in any church is a strong junior high department. Junior high school is now the make-or-break time for children, in my opinion. Why? Because this is when peer pressures really take hold. So our best efforts and budgeting need to be aimed at doing a good job with kids in this age bracket.

If you will love and nurture boomer kids, they will love you. Not only that, if churches will take our junior highers seriously, we boomer parents will be loyal to you in return—and for years after we have run through the mill with them.

So, no more important step exists for any church than to develop a highly visible, highly effective junior high program that will reach significant numbers of boomer kids. Toward that end, an effective starter strategy for your church will be to gather all your junior high workers together and show them how vital they are, not only in the evangelization of the children, themselves, but also to the wider purpose of reaching, through the children, their parents and their communities.

Farfetched? Not at all. That's the way it goes now. In times past it was parents who brought their kids into the Kingdom. However, we may now be in a time when reverse evangelism is true. Certainly it is true in the case of Sharon whom you met earlier. Now meet also Dean and Char.

Dean

Dean was a quiet engineer type. I'd seen him in our services frequently for about three months before he asked to speak with me.

"I need to talk to you, Pastor," he began in a blunt tone.

"What can I do for you, Dean?"

"Pastor, how can I get faith?"

I'd never before talked to anyone so sincere about wanting to have faith. I asked him a question in return? "Well, what do you think faith is?"

"I'm not certain, but I'm tired of being left out," he answered, sounding exasperated.

"What exactly do you mean, Dean?"

"Well, every one of my kids has committed their lives to Christ and are reading their Bibles. Even our seven-year-old is. Their mother prays with them and I'm just left out.

"They don't make me feel bad or anything. In fact, they have been careful not to put pressure on me. But since they've been coming to this church, things have changed. I want in. I just can't figure out how to believe, though."

Dean has a very successful business and is a good father. Ordinarily, he's not a highly emotional person, but the day he spoke to me he appeared almost panicky. As I assessed his mental outlook, I decided he really was serious about his quest. I just didn't know what to say to him, however.

That Wednesday night, when we both knelt down, Dean accepted Christ into his life, and he's attending our church to this day. He didn't have a strong emotional experience

---

Remember, one of the best investments your church can make is in its children's ministry team, because these folks are touching the next generation of kids for Christ.

---

when he accepted Christ; he had already been indirectly evangelized through our children's ministry. Dean's kids had been taken seriously by him, for he couldn't deny that God was at work in their lives.

Char

Char is a single mom in our congregation who first came because her teenage daughter began attending Eastside Church. Char had weathered a bitter divorce a few years back, before she and her daughter found their way into our services. After she had attended for some time, she became a member.

Recently, I overheard someone ask her? "Char, how did you begin attending Eastside?"

"Well, my kids were going through a terribly rough time and I didn't want them to have to go back to church alone, though I was certain there weren't any churches who would really care about them. I figured they had been hurt enough without having some do-gooders attack them.

"Then one Sunday afternoon I came home and found my daughter just beaming. She said she had attended a church with one of her friends that morning 'where they even had guitars in the service.' She said the youth group was 'great' and the pastor was 'funny.'

"She also discovered that it was okay to be the child of a divorcée at Eastside. I can tell you that I was healed in just a few weeks."

We all laughed as she finished her story. Not wanting to leave it at that, she continued? "One of my kids thought the pastor looked a lot like Red Skelton, too."

I blushed as those present roared.

Char added, "I came because Eastside was a place that was meeting my kids' needs. I couldn't stay away. I could tell there was a sincere love for my kids here."

Boomer parents, in surprising numbers, are seriously considering returning to church for the sake of their kids. Char is just one more example of many I could give here. Suffice to say that, *in our time, reaching kids has to be at the heart of any growing church.*

ESSENTIALS OF A KID-SENSITIVE CHURCH

So where do you begin to develop a kid-sensitive environment that will appeal to us boomers and our sophisticated expectations for our kids? Let me walk you through what I believe are a few essentials, practical steps that can be instrumental in helping your church serve and minister to baby boomer parents:

Clean, Well-designed Children's Facilities

Design facilities that emphasize and appeal to children. Show by all that you do with your buildings and grounds that kids are a priority in your church. Then ensure that those facilities are always clean.

The first choice of a vacation destination for Americans is Disney World. When asked why, visitors said it was because they felt safe there. I wondered why they felt safe. On a recent visit I learned what the poll had discovered. This feeling of safety results from an extreme, even fanatic commitment to cleanliness.

If you've ever visited Disneyland or Disney World, you've no doubt noticed the hundreds of young people picking up paper cups and waste. These popular theme parks have to be the two cleanest places on earth. The cleanliness and attractiveness of your Sunday School classrooms will similarly speak volumes to us boomer parents.

"Visitor Friendly" Children's Facilities

Plan your children's facilities so that they are "visitor friendly." That is, make it easy for visiting families to find where to take their children. Nothing is more disturbing to a visitor parent than having to wander confused around an unfamiliar church, looking for the place where their children are to worship. Whatever children's facilities you have, a sufficient number of guides or greeters should be strategically placed in large enough numbers to spot bewildered visitors.

Trained, Gifted Teachers

The only circumstance worse than no children's ministry is a ministry staffed by people who are there only because the pastor badgered them into it. Churches would be better off offering fewer services if they can't staff their programs with dedicated, enthusiastic people. Attracting teachers is a gift. And gifted people attract other gifted people.

So offer effective training for Sunday School teachers and children's church workers. Any well-stocked bookstore will have plenty of terrific resources available to help you. If you don't find any on the shelf, ask the store owner to guide you through their catalogs.

Remember, one of the best investments your church can make is in its children's ministry team, because these folks are touching the next generation of kids for Christ. They are also, as we have noted, part of the greatest expression of evangelism in the Church.

Creative, Innovative Activities

Baby boomers love innovation, especially when it means that our kids will experience creative activities. Any imaginative effort out of the ordinary is attractive and appreciated. We will watch for it.

Children's ministries, more than any other, present marvelous opportunities for creative people to use their special abilities. Many besides teachers can serve here. For, along with teachers, artistic, talented people are also needed to build props and equipment and to create exciting experiences for the kids.

For a time, we had our Sunday School greeters wear Disney character outfits. Some even put together biblical character costumes. The parents loved it even more than the kids.

I know of a church in Spokane, Washington, that is having tremendous success in reaching baby boomers. Every Halloween they put on a community "experience" at the local arena. They set up games and booths with biblical themes that attract as many as 9,000 kids and parents in one evening? That such a church is perceived to be "family friendly" is no accident.

Remember, any attempt to be creative will always be appreciated. Past church experience tends to be so short on imaginative projects, that any attempt to improve that experience will cause you to stand out.

Positive Pastoral Comments

Appropriate pastoral comments about parenting and the need to minister to our kids positively are very helpful. Nothing is worse than the pastoral guilt trip, so avoid it. The high calling of ministering to kids should be spoken about often by church leaders without attaching guilt to it.

I make it a rule never to mention our children's ministry when we need workers. I wait until we're well stocked, then I thank the workers and ask our church to join me in showing them our appreciation.

It's a wonderful practice as well to honor the workers who serve well in the kids' area. All who serve in whatever way should be thanked and honored for their contributions to this vital ministry. At Eastside Church, we give out several plaques a year on Sunday mornings to honor workers in our Children's Church.

THE BOOMER CHURCH EVOLVES

Our picture of Harry Boomer's church is growing and expanding. He sees that it has Disneyland-quality experiences for his kids, along with a welcome input of singles in leadership. And everything is kept casual, upbeat and extremely practical.

Harry glances at his bulletin and also notices that this church holds meetings on Thursday nights for recovering addicts. He, a recovering alcoholic himself, is intrigued. The announcement tells him that this congregation genuinely welcomes addicted people and expects them to be attending church here. Harry decides to attend that Thursday night meeting and check it out for himself.

In the next chapter, let's talk about how this program and others like it can work in any local church.

6

THE SPECTRUM OF ADDICTION

"It is for freedom that Christ has set us free. Stand firm, then, and do not let yourselves be burdened again by a yoke of slavery."
—Galatians 5:1

"Looking at him is painful. A 14-year addiction to heroin has caused David [Crosby] to resemble a Bowery bum. The spiritual leader of the Woodstock nation is now a vision of decay."
—Edward Kirsch[1]

THE anthem of the '60s was "Try it; you'll like it." The freedom to experiment and experience the full spectrum of human sensuality was considered a birthright, as far as we baby boomers were concerned. That this experiment has soured for our entire generation has been well documented.

ADDICTION WEARS MANY FACES

Drug Addiction

As I entered the home of the once-great NBA (National Basketball Association) star, I could hardly believe what I saw: The bedroom curtains were almost entirely burnt; the dresser, bedspread and carpet were also burnt. Thick soot clung to the ceiling. We took pictures of the bizarre scene, hoping for an opportunity to use them to intervene for Jerry (not his real name).

Susan (not her real name), his wife, was frantic when she saw the room. Obviously, Jerry had been free-basing cocaine, and the fix had fallen onto the floor, setting the carpet on fire, which then ignited the entire bedroom.

In a shrill, pain-filled voice, Susan screeched, "They [Jerry and his nephew] didn't even bother to call the fire department! He could have been put in prison for murder this time! Every one in this building could have burned up!"

Pausing to catch her breath, she went on, "All they did was throw water on it—he and his nephew. They just closed the door, then moved to the next room to take more drugs!"

The basement bathroom was another sight to behold. The floor was covered with soot from free-basing cocaine. By the evidence, Jerry had practically lived in the bathroom, concocting a mixture of ether and cocaine, inhaling it and experiencing the short but intense high. I wiped my finger across the floor and couldn't believe my eyes.

"He must have spent hours in here," I commented to Ron, a member of our ministry team, and to Susan as we walked through the house, taking inventory.

Holes had been kicked in the walls of other rooms. The kitchen also bore mute evidence of his ceaseless binges. Two NCAA (National Collegiate Athletic Association) Most Valuable Player awards in basketball and a number of trophies were shoved into a corner. Jerry had certainly lost touch with his real self. These symbols of past acclaim and respect were all he had left to hold on to.

Tears welled up in my eyes. I'd met few people with as wonderful a personality as Jerry's. His intelligence was far above average and his athletic prowess was equal to any, but the white powder had reduced him to subhuman levels.

Jerry started snorting cocaine while playing on one of the more notable NBA teams in the nation. Up to that point, like many of his generation, he'd experimented only with marijuana. First, his use of cocaine was just for recreation. After all, it was the mid-1970s, the era of widespread drug experimentation.

I'd been there too. However, I had the good fortune to end my experimentation approximately eight years before he had—before drugs were as pervasive as they are now.

Jerry and Susan had called our church for help, as they didn't know where else to turn. I'd first seen Jerry shortly after reading about his problem on the front page of the local paper. They had attended our Easter Sunday service, at which time they both committed their lives to Jesus Christ. I didn't see them for a number of months after that.

Then, one day, I received a frantic call from Susan asking me to spend some time with Jerry, as he was in jail for rearranging her jaw. She had done the right thing by calling the police and having Jerry charged with assault. We hoped this would bring him to his senses. The next few months taught me a great deal about the varieties and levels of addiction that inhabit the upper echelons of my generation.

The addiction level in Jerry's life was so intense and the co-dependent behavior of Susan so strong, we prayed daily that the Lord would lead them to freedom from the bondage of drugs. I began to take the addiction issue more seriously myself. I'm also happy to report that Jerry is doing better now, after multiple trips to treatment clinics, and I know Christ is at work in him.

Sexual Addiction

The sexual promiscuity that has permeated every strata of our culture is a reflection of the campuses of the 1960s. And a further reflection is the sexual addiction that is now as much a reality to the baby boomer generation as is the addiction to drugs and alcohol. The boomer generation is intimately involved in all these addictive cycles.

The free-love movement, along with an openness toward new models of sexual expression, set up an entire generation for the most severe kinds of sexual problems. All that, coupled with readily accepted serial marriages, has led to high instances of incest, sexual perversions and personality disorders.

In *Out of the Shadows*, Dr. Patrick Carnes very clearly addresses the tragedy of sexual addictions. Unfortunately, however, this aspect of ministry life is rarely considered or taken seriously by the Church. Yet any congregation that seeks to reach the boomers must be ready to deal with the fallout of a generation's sexual promiscuity and experimentations.

Meet John (not his real name), a trusted brother in our congregation. On a busy spring day, three weeks earlier, John had called me for an appointment. I had no idea what he wanted to talk about, though I knew it was important.

> *I don't think anybody anticipated in the early 1970s that pastors in the 1990s would have to be adept at dealing with terminal diseases related to sexual addictions and drug experimentation.*

Even so, as our church was involved in a building expansion program just then, and my time was very scarce, I hadn't been able to invest much prayer in this meeting today with John.

In John's case, I suspected only minor marital problems, so was not at all prepared for the bomb he was about to drop on me. As he sat down, I reached out, playfully cuffed his shoe and asked, "How can I help you, John?"

Then I noticed his saddened eyes, his quivering lower lip, and I realized the scene was about to get intense. I'll have to admit that—as other pastors have undoubtedly experienced—these thoughts passed through my mind: *It*

*looks like I better figure on at least 45 minutes for this. I hope
I have the energy for it.*

I soon discovered that I would need about an hour-and-
a-half to allow John the opportunity to talk through his
deep, painful secret. Pressing his teeth into his lower lip, he
launched into his incredible confession: "Pastor, I've gotten
into the habit of seeing prostitutes again."

I was shocked right down to my toes! I wasn't ready for
this one. But I had to make certain I didn't show my surprise, lest it intimidate him from speaking freely.

"And now I've got a serious venereal disease, Pastor.
I've contracted a terrible case of herpes, and I'm going to
have to go home this evening and tell Jan (not her real
name)! What'll I do?"

We both decided it would be best if he did tell Jan
immediately. We scheduled another appointment for him
the following morning. Subsequent counseling appointments were also necessary for a number of months.

That first day we discussed John's behavioral history.
John's sexual experiences had started in the mid-1960s on
campus during the free-love movement. His activities were
very broad, yet consistent with the image of that era.

Though he had lived as a Christian now for about nine
years, he'd never quite erased the impact of his "dark
years." Healing in John's case not only entailed restoring
and healing his home relationships, but taking him back in
time to recover from the damages of his early adult sexual
experimentations.

AIDS

Trina (not her real name) met with me after an evening service in which I'd given a message on the Church's reaction
to the AIDS crisis. We had just recently buried a young man
who belonged to our church. Six years before that he had a

three-month fling in the homosexual community where he contracted AIDS. We also knew of several others who had tested positive to the HIV virus.

My message dealt with our church encouraging a compassionate response to AIDS, and I gave instructions to those who felt they might be susceptible to this sinister virus that has spread so rapidly through several strata of American society. I also encouraged our church to understand the AIDS crisis in a scientific sense in order to avoid some of the speculation and sensationalism that so often accompanies the Christian quest.

Tearfully, Trina said, "Pastor, thank you for that message tonight. Thank you also for making me feel accepted."

I had no idea that Trina had been infected with the AIDS virus, although I did know that she had been an intravenous drug user when she met the Lord in our church. Immediately I introduced her to one of our pastoral care staff for prayer. Later I discovered that Trina had contracted AIDS by sharing a hypodermic needle with her roommate, who thereafter died from this disease.

Trina remains a viable part of our congregation and has shared her unfortunate experience at various school assemblies and discussed the real threat of the AIDS virus to the drug community. Today, Trina is taking the experimental drug, AZT, which seems to be helping. We have not, in any way, pointed out to the entire church that she is an AIDS sufferer, but have continued, as a staff, to pray and intercede for her and to help her in any way we can.

It was at this same time that Don (not his real name) came to talk to me. Don, the father of four children, had moved from a nearby community to attend our church because he'd been told he would be "safe" here.

Don's problem was bisexuality. And, as with many in the bisexual community, he was susceptible to flings in "john toilets." Although a Christian for 17 years, he had, for a short time, due to frustration and anger about an unsatisfactory home life, become involved in homosexual experiments at massage parlors and shopping mall rest rooms.

It was during this short fling that he contracted AIDS and had been diagnosed as carrying the HIV virus for about two years before he began attending our church. He could hardly bring himself to speak to me.

Haltingly, he began: "Pastor, would you just pray with me, please. I have the terminal disease you've read about. I also have four wonderful kids. I love them and I work hard for them.

"I just recently got a promotion to a management level position in our corporation, and I'm afraid to tell them that I have AIDS, though my wife knows about it. We've decided to live together platonically and seek to grow in the Lord together."

Thankfully, his wife had not contracted the virus as well. Don's plight was truly tragic. He had sought counseling and dealt with his homosexual tendencies three years earlier with true repentance and forgiveness. And though he had walked soundly and solidly in the Lord for that three-year period, he now had to face the fact that he had contracted a dreaded terminal disease during that unfortunate three-month lapse.

ADDICTS IN THE CHURCH?

These incidences really jarred me into reality. No seminary class had ever prepared me to deal with these issues. Quite honestly, I don't think anybody anticipated in the early 1970s that pastors in the 1990s would have to be adept at dealing with terminal diseases related to sexual addictions and drug experimentation. Though these concerns were highly unlikely in the past, now in today's permissive society, we in the Church will find our boundaries increasingly encroached upon by the entire spectrum of addiction.

I shared the stories above only to break a myth—the myth that there are only a few, isolated cases of drug, alco-

---

The Church will have to adjust its view concerning sanctification and liberation from addictions or, every time an addict has a relapse, we'll throw him or her out of the Church as a backslider, thereby negating the full meaning of salvation.

---

hol or sexual addiction in churches, and that conversion will instantly deal with every aspect of addiction.

I also wish to dispel the myth that it will be the rare church who deals with these types of "problem people." The thirty something crowd is particularly desensitized to the threat of drugs and alcohol. So ary church dealing with the baby boom generation will have at least 30 to 40 percent of its congregation who have experimented significantly and have possibly had long-term involvements with drugs, alcohol or sexual aberrations.

In a culture where self-treatment by means of medications containing drugs and/or alcohol is encouraged through advertising over the airways, on billboards and in the media, there's a good possibility that even more of our population will become addicted by this means. This possibility, coupled with the highly permissive use of illicit drugs in our culture, contains a built-in potential for further instances of addiction.

That every substance-abuse addict, whether on alcohol or drugs, has an 85 percent chance of a periodic relapse is a fact. This statistic means the Church will have to adjust its view concerning sanctification and liberation from addictions or, every time an addict has a relapse, we'll throw him or her out of the Church as a backslider, thereby negating the full meaning of salvation. After all, would we not consider a hospital derelict in its mission, if—every time a patient relapsed—he or she were thrown out, rather than nursed back to health?

Congregations will need to network with recognized authorities on addictions and deal forthrightly with these issues in peoples' lives, even to survive as a church in the next few decades. For addicts need a safe place to go where they will be accepted and have the process of their freedom understood and appreciated.

MINISTERING TO ADDICTS

In this regard, I really believe that our congregation's experience with baby boomers and handling of their problems will become the norm—and already is the norm for many compassionate churches across the country.

One afternoon, at an impromptu staff gathering, we discussed the number of counseling appointments being made with alcoholics and drug addicts. We were carrying counseling loads far too heavy to continue and still remain sane or unaffected by them.

At first, we thought the word was getting out that we were the place to seek out if someone had an addiction problem. I even believed that our message of "loving, accepting and forgiving" those the Lord brought to our gatherings had inadvertently set us up for ministering to an inordinate number of addicts and alcoholics. I've since concluded that neither is the case. I really think we are more likely a reflection of what is truly happening in our society.

Ron Rearick—the former Mafia hit man known as "Iceman" and now one of our staff members—was seeing as many as eight drug addicts a day. Leaning forward at the conference table, he confided, "I don't know if I can carry on with this kind of load much longer. We've got to do something, Doug."

Talking to at least eight alcoholics a week, I replied: "Yeah, I'm fried myself." And being aware that approximately 20 percent of our population are genetically predisposed to alcoholism, I could see my case load continuing to grow.

So John suggested, "Why don't we start our own AA [Alcoholics Anonymous] meetings. This would reduce the time pressure on us, and we would probably be more effective. I've found that addicts are the best people to help addicts."

We acted on this ministry suggestion immediately. At first, we called the program "Born to Choose Ministries," naming it after Ron's outreach in school assemblies and churches. This program has subsequently grown, is now titled "Lifeline" and meets every Thursday night.

Our Lifeline Support Program currently numbers several hundred people a week. We now have additional support groups: Al-Anon (a group growing out of AA for nonalcoholic friends and relatives of alcoholics), ACOA (Adult Children of Alcoholics) and a group for people with eating disorders, as well as another for those with sexual addictions and distortions, called the Agape Group. Our support groups have some weaknesses, but these are outnumbered by their many strengths—and we improve weekly.

We're also implementing plans to provide intervention in these areas. Anyone who has ministered extensively to addicts knows that only a few of them will admit they have a problem. Thus, intervention is often essential to save those who are abusing high-powered drugs or are sustaining high levels of alcoholism. In such cases, when the levels of abuse are so high, the instances of successful intervention are few indeed. In other words, even before these people hit bottom, their addictions will kill them.

Even though we've been involved in these support programs for only three years, we're finding that the process of programming a ministry to the addicted is a developing and changing one. But in all of it, I feel that our greatest strength in ministering to the addicted is our willingness to talk intelligently and nonhysterically about the factors of addiction.

Some of the things we have discovered have now been modeled in other large churches across the country. Rather than being the exception, AA meetings will become the norm in boomer churches. The dysfunctions of this generation will weaken any church that does not reach out to address these all-important issues of alcoholism and drug addiction. After all, how can we become loving, effective forces for Christ's Kingdom if we can never shake the monkeys off our own backs?

One of our pastors, Dr. Larry Shelton, recently spoke to a group of ministers in our area, one of whom approached Larry and said, "I hear you're involved at Eastside Church now."

Larry turned and replied: "Yes, I am, and enjoying it a great deal."

The young minister continued. "I understand they have a large number of dysfunctional people in that church."

Larry chuckled about this and excitedly reported back to our staff: "Doesn't that ["a large number of dysfunctional people"] sound like the kind of crowd Jesus would hang out with? I'm proud to be here!"

Another staff member also shared some comments from a community worker who came to our site to check out some new construction: "Watch out! Those people up there let anyone who has diseases or all sorts of problems come around. You never know what you're going to run into."

At first, our staff member was reluctant to tell him that he, too, attended our church, lest the worker would think ill of him. Eventually, however, our guy found the courage not only to tell the worker where he attended, but to invite him to one of our services!

PRACTICAL SUGGESTIONS

These suggestions are for any congregation choosing to reach out to dysfunctional people of my boomer generation:

1. *Initiate occasions when specific sermons/messages address various addictions.* In this way you can help addicts:

- to recognize their problems before they reach bottom, before the addiction results in serious, permanent damage. For them to come out of denial is the first vital step.
- to realize that the spiritual issue of being freed from addiction is best addressed by receiving the gospel and walking in the open with Christ.

- to know the value of walking with a congregation, for getting involved in the lives of others helps break the destructive patterns shaped by the very addictive forces that have been dominant in their lives.

2. *Develop a theology of Christian growth that allows for the healing process of addictive cycles in individuals.* To attach the assurance of one's salvation to one's ability to overcome an addiction is a mistake and wrong—one that will be very harmful!

3. *Be adventurous in your church's outreach, extending care to the hurting and addicted segments of your community.* Make known to your people that you welcome those with addictions and also that, while some experience instant healing, you are aware other healings do take time. Let it be known that, in any case, you stand ready to minister Christ's love to them.

4. *Establish programs of our own, even if your church is small.* I would venture to say that any church which will begin its own AA program of, say, even a hundred in number will quickly find that its community will perceive that congregation as being a people in touch with real needs.

5. *Engage in networking, if your church is not large enough to commence programs of its own.* Every community has experts in many areas of concern.

For instance, we've found that care units and many clinics dealing with addictions have been more than willing to help us out for free and are open to networking with us. Every pastor should have information on these clinics in their community. They ought to know, at least on an acquaintance basis, people who deal with detoxification, for instance.

It would be well also to network with groups that can help you deal with homosexual people. Homosexuals Anonymous or Metanoya Ministries are extremely helpful in this area of concern.

6. *Educate your congregation to expect people with AIDS in their midst.* Such preparation is vital, for all successful ministry grows out of the personal attitudes of those who comprise it.

7. *Read and encourage others to read the various books offered in the following bibliography:*

Carnes, Patrick, Ph.D. *Out of the Shadows: Understanding Sexual Addiction.* Minneapolis, MN: CompCare Publishers, 1985.

Kritsberg, Wayne. *The Adult Children of Alcoholics Syndrome.* Deerfield Beach, FL: Health Communications, Inc., 1986.

Larsen, Earnie. *Stage Two Recovery: Life Beyond Addiction.* New York: Harper & Row, 1985.

Martin, Sara Hines. *Healing for Adult Children of Alcoholics.* Nashville: Broadman Press, 1988.

Myers, David G. *Social Psychology.* New York: McGraw-Hill Book Co., 1983. Contains excellent chapters on addiction.

Simon, Sidney, D.Ed. *Getting Unstuck.* New York: Warner Books, 1988.

Wegscheider-Cruse, Sharon. *The Miracle of Recovery: Healing for Addicts, Adult Children and Co-Dependents.* Deerfield Beach, FL: Health Communications, Inc., 1989.

Woititz, Janet Garringer. *Adult Children of Alcoholics.* Deerfield Beach, FL: Health Communications, Inc., 1983.

Woititz, Janet G. *Struggle for Intimacy.* Deerfield
Beach, FL: Health Communications, Inc., 1985.

Okay, now your church has evolved into a loving,
accepting, forgiving congregation, the safest place in the
world for the dysfunctional person to seek help. But once
he or she has found Christ and is walking with the Lord,
what place will that person have in your church?

Will this new Christian quickly become just one of many
or be fully authenticated and celebrated as an individual in
his or her own right? And are opportunities for service and
leadership real or imagined?

In the next chapter, let's look at the importance of the
individual in the boomer church.

Note
1. Edward Kirsch, "The Death of David Crosby," *SPIN Magazine, People* magazine.

7
CELEBRATING THE INDIVIDUAL

When you see us boomers coming through your
doors, remember that we think like consumers.
You may not like it nor agree with it, but you'll
understand us a whole lot better if you learn to
look at us from a consumer perspective.
—Doug Murren

EVEN by conventional American standards, we baby boomers are highly individualistic and highly distrustful of conformist cultures. The anthems of nonconformity have followed us from the 1960s into the 1990s, ensuring that the celebration of individualism is still a vital part of the value systems we've carried into mid-life.

WE'RE INDIVIDUALS, NOT NUMBERS

We distrust anything that even appears to threaten an individual's rights. We are skeptical of anything that is monolithic. We are fearful of being part of any mass movement.

Perhaps it had something to do with going through junior high and high school in such overcrowded conditions, we're all fearful of simply becoming a number again. This kind of talk is quite prevalent among us boomers. We don't want to be just numbers or swallowed up in some impersonal system.

Our distrust applies particularly to institutions. Asked, in 1985, by the Gallup Poll to rate the list of 10 social and political institutions according to their trustworthiness, without references to their leaders, baby boomers emerged as the least trusting of all age groups toward eight of these institutions: organized religion, the military, banks and banking, public school, Congress, newspapers, big business and organized labor.[1]

Obviously then, only those organizations that exist for the individual will succeed with boomers in the '90s. Those institutions that expect the individual to bend are likely to turn us off.

WE HAVE A CONSUMER PERSPECTIVE

The average boomer is a consummate consumer—even when it comes to religion. We've been reared as the focus of the advertising sector of our society; the media have aimed at us and so has the military. We've been taught to look for products and services that interest us the most. We tend to view churches from this perspective as well.

Here, in Seattle, where I'm writing, we have a chain of stores called Nordstrom. You've probably already heard of them, for they are famous as the ultimate stores for the individual. Customers can actually return merchandise they bought 10 years before—if they have the audacity to do so—and receive new merchandise in exchange.

Obviously, part of the reason for the success of the Nordstrom stores is their famed appreciation of the individual; they appeal to this need in us to be valued as persons. That's why Nordstrom's customers are not faceless entities; all are individuals—each with a recognizable face and distinctive tastes.

Unlike the Church, Nordstrom's recognizes and appeals to the perspective of the consumer. We church leaders aren't very good at thinking about church life from a consumer's perspective. In fact, this concept makes many of my church friends angry. It's a perspective that doesn't really matter, they say.

Nevertheless, that's the way we thirty something people are thinking—as consumers—when we look for a church. So when we visit your church, we are asking these kinds of questions:

- Does this church take me seriously as an individual?
- Do they remember my name?
- Will this place meet my needs?

- What services do they offer me and my family?
- Is this church interested in me or interested only in its self-preservation?

To reach boomers, churches will have to go overboard, emphasizing the fact that the Church exists for the individu-

---

Unchurched boomers particularly don't like being told what to think. We will value, instead, a church that is highly appreciative of multiple opinions—a congregation that honors each individual's right to think on his or her own.

---

al. Let me illustrate this basic line of thinking, which I personally believe squares more accurately with the biblical concept of ministering to people. Imagine a Sunday morning appeal from the pastor, one that is typical of those in many evangelical churches in America, it goes something like this:

"We need 20 people to work in the nursery. May I have a show of 20 hands of those who will volunteer? After all, this can't be a strong church if we don't have these 20 workers in our nursery."

Now, that sort of appeal is the antithesis of what would evoke a response from consumer-minded boomers. Let me illustrate what would work far better with boomers:

"Good morning! We're happy you could all be here today. I want to remind you that this church is interested in each gift and each individual in this congregation.

"Tonight we'll give you an opportunity to discover your spiritual gifts in a special class that's being offered. We hope your gifts will find expression in our congregation, as we have many opportunities for service here. We have a list of opportunities to serve that may appeal to your basic orientation. We're interested in your gifts being released here."

Do you see the subtle difference? In the first appeal, the pastor was asking people to match themselves up with needs "our church" had. In the second appeal, they're valuing the gifts and passions that are already resident in people's hearts. This perspective may seem subtle to some, but it is very evident to most of us boomers.

So when you see us boomers coming through your doors, remember that we think like consumers. You may not like it nor agree with it, but you'll understand us a whole lot better if you learn to look at us from a consumer perspective.

WE RESPECT INDIVIDUAL OPINIONS

Respecting the opinions of others is very important to us boomers. As a boomer pastor myself, I've learned the hard way that, even though I feel strongly about matters that are clearly in line with the Scriptures, I still need to be careful about how I share them. If I don't treat respectfully those who have opinions counter to mine, I will quickly lose the ear of my constituency.

Also, if you're going to pastor boomers, you won't get away with trying to give us processed opinions. If we come to your church and it's obvious that we'll be handed opinions on a variety of issues, we'll feel threatened by such an environment. We just aren't interested in anyone giving us processed opinions, as is done in those churches that tell us what to believe about everything—from the Iran-Contra scandal to the number of children we should have. That's one of the reasons we've stayed away so long.

So no one had better underestimate our high regard for individual opinions and freedoms. Jerry Falwell may have spoken for the conservative constituency of his generation well enough, but I have the feeling that we boomers won't have any such spokespersons.

Unchurched boomers particularly don't like being told what to think. We will value, instead, a church that is highly appreciative of multiple opinions—a congregation that honors each individual's right to think on his or her own. Baby boomers like this perspective on Christian growth. We simply want to be given the right tools to make good decisions. We don't want our decisions made for us.

My own view of pastoral leadership has helped me in this area. I don't believe it's helpful to give people prepackaged forms of Christianity. It really hasn't worked in the past, and I feel it will be even less effective in the future.

I'm truly convinced that the gospel can work effectively in this kind of an environment. In fact, it will work better when people are encouraged to formulate opinions for themselves based on the Scriptures that have been given to them. I believe they will then stand more committed to what they believe.

Churches aren't going to fare any better than unions if they expect to exist without appreciating the growth process and value of every individual. Now, you say, "Hey, wait a minute? Isn't that what church is all about—creeds and doctrines? The individual existing for the Church, the organization?"

Well, maybe, to some extent. But if you want to appeal to boomers, remember that we won't be greatly concerned about whether your denomination succeeds or not. So, please, don't talk about denominational projects. We're just not interested. And don't talk to us about your institutional needs. We won't be impressed. To be frank, we really don't care.

On the other hand, show us a person or family who needs help and we'll be right there. Wholeheartedly involved, we'll help an individual. But save an institution or help an institution? Not a chance!

We boomers are ready to be tapped, but *not* for someone else's vision. We'd rather give our hearts and time—after all, boomers already volunteer an average of four hours a week to charitable works—to those who recognize our gifts and let us be part of their Christian team.

So talk first about our passions and our gifts, and we'll keep coming back. Encourage us to allow the Holy Spirit to release us in areas that excite us—and we'll make your church a success!

WE DON'T SEEK CONSENSUS

On a recent, sunny, spring afternoon, my wife, Debbie, and I stood in our church parking lot, awaiting the arrival of a local political candidate. She had asked to meet with us about some particular community concerns she had.

As she drove up in her Oldsmobile sedan, Deb turned to me and asked, "What do you suppose she wants?"

"I suppose she wants me to ensure our congregation's vote for her next election," I answered, laughing as I spoke.

"Boy, is she going to be surprised? I think you're a great pastor, but I don't think we really want you telling us how to vote."

As we strolled through our church building with the candidate, she expressed her Christian values and her commitment to the community. Repeatedly she stated her hope that we could be partners together to make our community all it could be.

When we were seated in the makeshift conference room in our new building, I felt I not only needed to express my support, but also fill her in on our church's particular temperament. I decided I would give my explanation whenever she approached the real purpose of her visit. Then, as she was about to ask me to encourage our church to vote for her, I began:

"Dorothy, I really like your approach. But if you were to come to our services some Sunday morning, you would see very young to middle-aged folks who are all highly individualistic. You see, people here like to form their own opinions. They respect mine, but I can't really get away with giving my opinion as our church's position on any issue.

"We've trained our people to value their right to their own opinions and to respond accordingly. You see, most of us are baby boomers who resent institutions telling us what to believe. We'll be as helpful as we can, however."

Though my frankness possibly surprised her, Dorothy responded graciously, and the parting was friendly. Even though we are a large church in this area, we didn't represent a massive constituency for her anyway, because of the diversity of opinions—political and otherwise—held within our congregation. I'm sure this variety of viewpoints within a congregation is true of many American churches today, especially so of baby boomer churches.

I wouldn't even try to get a consensus from our church on most nonessential issues. Once we get beyond the infallibility of the Scriptures, the lordship of Jesus Christ, the triune God, and the orthodox statements about the Apostles'

Creed, I'm very careful not to assert opinions that are too strong. Rather, we strive to maintain an atmosphere for people where the process of growth is encouraged and celebrated.

WE LIKE MULTIPLE OPTIONS

For several years now, we've had multiple service times. We've had Friday night services, Saturday night services and, at times, six different services on Sundays. We held this schedule both because of the constant, rapid growth in our congregation and because of our facility's limitations.

But along the way, I made a discovery: People like a church with multiple service times. Why? Well, originally I thought it was due to the appearance of success. I was wrong. People like multiple options for services, because it states, loud and clear, that we want to adjust to YOUR schedule. In other words, *we're interested in serving YOU!*

If the boomer sees a church with multiple service times, she or he thinks, *Hey, this is like Denny's and 7-Eleven. They want to serve ME. I don't have to fit their schedule. They're giving me several options, depending on what's happening in my week. That's great!*

When speaking to groups planning to start new churches, I've said with sincere conviction that *I would start off with at least two morning service times the very first Sunday I open the doors.*

Not only do people's schedules demand options today, but multiple services speak in the cultural language of our time. An organization that makes me fit my schedule to theirs sends a negative message to me. A schedule without options tells me I'm going to serve the organization.

Grocery stores and restaurants that are open 24 hours a day may not justify being open from, say, 2:00 to 4:00 A.M., but, perceptually, they're speaking volumes to the communities they serve. And so do churches that offer multiple service times. A flexible worship schedule also makes practical sense, as the cost is prohibitive today for the construction of facilities large enough for a single combined worship service each week.

The '90s are already shaping up to be the decade of servant leadership, a decade in which the laity will clearly be the driving force of the Church.

Recently a reporter visited our congregation on a Sunday morning to observe our services and to take photos. She met me the following week, and I was mildly surprised that she wanted to share her observations with me before they were printed. She made it clear that she wasn't a Christian and that, initially, she hadn't come as a "friendly" observer. Toward the end of our conversation, she finally confessed her own opinion of our services when she said, "I really enjoyed myself."

"Great! We really wouldn't want bad press, would we?" I replied, chuckling.

"You have so many different meeting times and options for people. I was pleasantly surprised. You really do care about people, don't you?" she asked, showing her surprise.

"Yes, we really do. There are a lot of different kinds of people in our church. We're mostly baby boomers and their kids, but we come in all sizes and ages."

"I was amazed that you had kids dressed in torn jeans sitting next to people in suits, yet no one seemed to be bothered by the other."

A hint of shock was evident in her voice. She had obviously waited all week to ask me how I felt about this.

Desiring to clarify the picture more, I added, "We highly value the individual. We try to make it clear that we're able to be ourselves. We're people with all kinds of opinions on all kinds of issues. But we all love Jesus and are committed to live a life that is consistent with the Bible."

That was the end of our conversation. With warm smiles for one another, we parted as friends. When her article was printed, it was a wonderful presentation of our church life in the Kirkland community.

WE PRACTICE SERVANT LEADERSHIP

The '90s are already shaping up to be the decade of servant leadership, a decade in which the laity will clearly be the driving force of the Church. By servant leadership, I don't mean passive leadership. Nor do I mean democratic leadership in the Church. Servant leadership, which Jesus modeled for us, is that which inspires and implements God's people to new personal heights they never thought imaginable.

This concept will have a great deal of appeal to boomers. We don't care to join any hot-shot church leader to fulfill his vision. We aren't very interested in building anyone's TV network or in erecting anyone's megachurch with the leader's portrait in the foyer of the sanctuary. Instead, we desire leadership where our individual gifts will be respected and released for good in the church that we attend.

I believe it's for this reason that we boomers are very difficult people to lead. We don't care to follow the "expert," marching in lockstep behind him. And corporations are finding this out.

Today's labor force is more like a volunteer force than like a corp of obedient employees. Boomers won't work just for a paycheck anymore. We need more incentive than that, such as being taken seriously as individuals. Otherwise, we're gone.

If this is true in the business environment, it's even more true when it comes to our place of worship. Not only will we joyfully embrace the gospel that celebrates our individuality as a gift from God. We will also serve enthusiastically alongside that church leader who helps us achieve *our* dreams.

Consequently, the '90s may well see a resurgence of John Wesley's discovery that the laity had to be released in order for the Church to become truly expanded. Even now, a grassroots movement of returning church leadership to lay persons is already growing and spreading in the evangelical Church.

We Are High on Personal Experience

As we have already seen, boomers are bringing about a whole new view of church leadership. The boomer church of the future:

- will have multiple options,
- will talk about the individual more than the institution,
- will maintain an atmosphere committed to truth, but respectful of counteropinions,
- will not try to force a consensus, and

- will exercise servant leadership that puts an individual's interests above the institution's needs.

That's quite a prescription for the churches in the 1990s decade ahead of us. But, as I view it, we really don't have any choice. So we establish a church environment that is boomer friendly, hospitable to singles and offering multiple service times.

But is it also experience-oriented?

Remember our friends, Bob and Betty Boomernosky whom we met in a previous chapter? They've just arrived at their church for morning worship. As they settle down in their chairs, Bob nudges Betty and observes, "Do you realize that they have three services today? We could have slept another half hour and made the next service."

Turning to Bob, Betty answers, "We'll have to remember that. Isn't that a great idea? Yes, I like this place already."

As the worship begins and Bob and Betty take each other's hand, an unusual Presence fills the meeting place, for the people gathered in this place really expect to encounter God here.

The churches who appeal to boomers will be high on personally experiencing spiritual realities, especially in worship services. Let's discuss next how that can happen.

Note
1. Paul C. Light, *Baby Boomers* (New York: W.W. Norton & Co., 1988), pp. 160-161.

8

IF IT IS REAL, I EXPECT TO EXPERIENCE IT!

"Follow the way of love and eagerly desire spiritual gifts, especially the gift of prophecy."
—1 Corinthians 14:1

A few weeks ago, while flipping through TV channels, I tuned in to one of the major network stations in Seattle. For a few moments, I found myself watching a local afternoon talk show. The host was interviewing a young man—a regular-looking guy—who claimed to be a spirit channeler. However, when he talked, he sounded like a leprechaun.

Here it was, the top of the afternoon, and I'm sitting and watching this guy act like Lord Somebody-or-Other from the thirteenth century. What actually caught my attention, however, wasn't just how ridiculous the guy sounded, but how seriously the studio audience was taking him. I couldn't believe it. Somehow, I couldn't imagine my folks watching this sort of nonsensical stuff.

EXPERIENCE: THE ULTIMATE TEST OF REALITY

What has changed in our culture to make possible and credible today—at least to some of those who were observing it—a TV show such as that I just described? Remember that the 1960s were a decade driven by a radical shift in worldview. And that shift, reflected today in boomer views of religion, changed dramatically the way our generation perceives spirituality and spiritual experience.

As products of what we boomers consider a highly spiritualized, experience-directed age, we thirty something people continue to look for and expect experiences in the spiritual realm. Admittedly, in the course of this search, unchurched boomers have become deeply interested in and oriented toward Far Eastern religious views—far more so than are our parents. We boomers so inclined may not have the effigies in or on our homes that Easterners do, but we still share with them a belief—unspecific though it may be—in the realm of the unseen.

What we are observing now in the New Age religions of the '80s and '90s is a full flowering of the experiential views that began blossoming in the late '60s. Timothy Leary's cry of "Turn On, Tune In, Drop Out" was not just a singular voice on the horizons of that era. He articulated the mindset of an entire generation so desperate for personal experience that it sought synthetic stimulation and consciously altered states through drug experimentation.

The '60s represented a "religion" that glorified personal experience with an emphasis on *individual, personal* experiences. And the anthems that then heralded such views were many. "Whatever turns you on" and "If it feels good, do it" reflected a faith of feeling. Though the boomer perspective today has become somewhat more sophisticated than during that time, this viewpoint emphasizing the need to experience, to feel, still remains with us.

BOOMERS HUNGER FOR SPIRITUAL EXPERIENCES

Any church group that wants to reach the boomer world will have to deal effectively with their overall cultural hunger for personal experiences. George Gallup confirmed this in his 1988 study. Gallup, in the October 1988 issue of his research bulletin, *Emerging Trends*, produced jointly with Princeton University, asserted throughout that the Church must realize the high expectation of personal experiences desired and expressed by the unchurched returning to church.[1]

Gallup contrasted studies conducted in 1962 with more recent polls dealing with spiritual experiences: "Twenty percent of those polled [in 1962] said that they had a religious experience."[2]

The next Gallup survey on this topic was conducted in 1976. This study showed that 31 percent of those interviewed said they had significant spiritual experiences.

We want, as a generation, to move beyond philosophical discussions of religions to the actual experience of God in our lives. The boomer heart, like every human heart, has always cried out for a personal experience with God.

The latest study in 1988 showed that, among even the unchurched, 35 percent stated that they had had significant spiritual experiences. This is an increase of 15 percent over the past 26 years.

Gallup concluded his brief report with a strong admonition to churches to accept and promote a belief in personal spiritual experiences.

MARKETING EXPERIENCE TO BOOMERS

Marketers know boomers will buy experience. Unlike our elders and youngsters, who tend to buy for quality or status, we want to *feel* it. For instance, stereo companies sell their goods to us by showing a listener with his winter muffler flapping from the sheer force of the sound coming from his stereo speakers.

Mazda sold its new 1990 model with a media blitz high on experience. One TV ad even let us ride with the driver, who was hooked up to an arsenal of sensor devices, each device recording what he was "feeling" when he drove. The ad's punch line was: "We know what you want to experience."

If Madison Avenue understands this fact that boomers seek experience, then the Church needs to also. Don't underestimate the impact of our worldview on us middle-aged boomers. If you talk religion to us, we expect to receive a spiritual experience of the living God.

We want, as a generation, to move beyond philosophical discussions of religions to the actual experience of God in our lives. The boomer heart, like every human heart, has always cried out for a personal experience with God.

A theology that is strong on personally experiencing God in one's life through a personal encounter with Jesus Christ will appeal to boomers. Churches today also need to reconsider if their liturgy celebrates such personal experience in their services.

THE NEED TO EXPERIENCE THE PRESENCE OF GOD

Yet to a lot of boomers considering a return to the Church, many of the churches we visit seem so sterile and antiseptic that they hardly hold our interest. Boomers, therefore, will demand an experience of God's presence in our lives before our generation will participate fully in the life of any church.

Let's join again our imaginary boomer couple, Bob and Betty Boomernosky. They are enjoying their return to church immensely. Bob is very impressed with how clean and attractive the children's Sunday School rooms are, even commenting to Betty about them. He thinks to himself: *The children's classes aren't anything like what I remember from childhood. They are far better!*

We boomers will determine the relative importance of your church on the basis of how you enable us to experience a personal, spiritual reality. Help us out. Share with us the Bible's guidelines for experiencing our faith and worship.

As the worship starts with songs of praise, Bob is pleasantly surprised how easy it is for him to sing along. He finds himself not only caught up in the joyful spirit of the people singing the songs, but actually participating. And, for just a moment, he is sure he felt God's presence while they were singing.

Before I began my message, I shared how I had sensed God's presence for the first time while I was a junior in college. Then I continued: "Some of you may be sensing God's presence for the first time today. It isn't exactly a feeling, but it *is* an experience. You know what I mean."

Bob knows what the pastor's saying all right. He's been wanting to have this kind of experience for a long time. Though certain it is possible, he's still surprised that he's experiencing it—a sense of the presence of God in his heart and life—today, his first time in church for many years.

As a self-confessed boomer and a Christian pastor, I'm one of those who's comfortable with a biblical faith that is high on personal experience. I believe we can individually experience God's Spirit and work in our lives. I believe that through a personal encounter with Jesus Christ, anyone can receive God in His fullness and be filled by Him. And I believe in the gift of the Holy Spirit because Jesus promised it (see John 14:16-17).

THE PENTECOSTAL/CHARISMATIC MOVEMENTS AND SPIRITUAL EXPERIENCE

It is a fact that Pentecostal and Charismatic groups are growing like wildfire in all sectors of the Church today. Why? A singular reason could be the fact that their theology is friendly toward spiritual experiences. Whether your congregation is Charismatic or not, much is to be learned from the impact that this movement has had on churches in the United States. For our population today lives in a worldview that is very open toward the manifestation of the unseen.

Admittedly, the Pentecostal/Charismatic movements may have had as much sociological as spiritual impetus in their growth. But the fact remains that they are high on the unseen workings in the spiritual realm, something that seems very plausible and, in fact, attractive to us boomers.

I'm a Charismatic Christian myself, and I believe my spiritual experiences in this area have been biblically guided and legitimately encountered. Even so, I certainly wouldn't expect everyone else to share my convictions.

Still, even though there has already been much theological discussion on this whole topic, I suggest we take advantage of the opportunity before us, as now presented by this post-war generation in search of spiritual experience to guide them into experiencing Christ as Lord and Savior with all that He offers to them. We really need to do a great deal more rethinking, even in Pentecostal/Charismatic circles, to allow those who are hungry for spiritual experiences to share in them legitimately and biblically.

EXPERIENCING PERSONAL SPIRITUAL REALITY: SENSING THE PRESENCE OF GOD

Remember, as we established earlier, we're the TV generation. And one of the impacts of being raised with television is that we expect to experience, in a multisense fashion, all of reality. The rock music we appreciate is designed to be felt. And for that reason, we regard The Who rock group as a sensory phenomenon.

True, the relative affluence of our parents allowed us time to pursue such sensory pursuits. But the fact remains that we have lived in this kind of world all our lives. From early childhood we've been taught the value of experience. And each new technical advance seems to bring a heightened appreciation for experiencing reality.

Consequently, we boomers will determine the relative importance of your church on the basis of how you enable us to experience a personal, spiritual reality. Help us out. Share with us the Bible's guidelines for experiencing our faith and worship.

Worship services that appeal to my generation have a strong sense of the presence of God. Whatever your brand or denomination, we need to have lots of talk and a high appreciation of the immediate presence of God.

But how do you handle a worship service that is high on personal experience? Here are a few practical suggestions that have helped me prepare for services that are high on spiritual experience:

1. Pray for it.
2. Desire spiritual gifts and manifestations of the Holy Spirit, as Paul suggested in 1 Corinthians 14:1.
3. Develop a faith environment that expects it.
4. Teach about it.
5. Have worship leaders who have a balanced understanding of the personal experience of God.
6. Develop a solid theological basis for such spiritual experiences.
7. Have a strategy and plan for the manifestation of Bible-based spiritual experiences in the Church that can be stated in the basic philosophy of your congregation.

   I've found that this prevents a great deal of confusion. If people know up front how you expect them to share and grow in their spiritual experiences, they are far more comfortable.
8. Make worship services a multidimensional experience. Worship services that release genuine opportunities for people to experience Christ personally involve, in most instances, imagination, as well as intellect.

RIVAL SPIRITUAL EXPERIENCES

Shortly after I met the Lord, a friend of mine named Dan also gave his heart to Christ. Previously, he had been deeply caught up in the drug culture of the late '60s and the early '70s. He'd also been moderately involved in Transcendental Meditation (TM) and various Eastern religions.

Yet, up to the time he left high school, Dan had been raised in church. What had happened to change him so? Dabbling in the occult and drugs was simply his rebellious attempt to abandon the faith of his parents.

Soon after his conversion, Dan shared with me the astonishing story of a deeply personal spiritual experience he had had a short time before. One day at the office, a Christian businessman friend who had known Dan all his life shared his own conversion with Dan. As a result, Dan became convinced to give his life anew to Christ and was invited to pray about it right there in the office.

Dan accepted.

But then, as the businessman took hold of Dan's hand to lead him back to the Lord, Dan said he began to hear voices in his mind. To his astonishment, as they prayed, one of the voices suddenly spoke aloud through Dan's voice, speaking the most blasphemous things imaginable, thereby preventing Dan from declaring Christ as his Lord. This outburst greatly startled both men.

Pausing for a moment, then recalling that, in the Scriptures, Jesus had commanded evil spirit entities to leave people, Dan's friend spoke in a firm voice: "In the name of Jesus, you cannot stop Dan from being freed in Christ!"

Immediately, Dan felt something leave him. Both of them were again startled as Dan experienced full release, for he could immediately pray freely. He said it was as though the real Dan had been buried under a heavy layer of lead and concrete. Then suddenly, that oppressive weight was gone.

However you may feel about this story or whether your theology allows for such manifestations is not the issue here. My point in sharing this strange story is that I've found Dan's experience is not at all unusual in our time, particularly on the West Coast. Because of intense dabbling in and experimenting with the occult, such experiences have become a surprisingly common phenomena, even among groups not necessarily looking for such experiences.

This acceleration of occult experiences, I believe, is a manifestation of people's hunger to experience the spiritual realm, regardless of the path it takes. In confirmation, we've witnessed firsthand a number of people in our congregation being freed from devil worship, as well as from the occult and New Age spiritual experiences.

Ministering to people illicitly introduced to the spiritual realm through demonic or occult encounters requires an environment that is comfortable with the vital and powerful experience of the Christian faith. These people will never be satisfied with simple platitudes or a list of doctrinal beliefs. If we are not poised to accept the reality of the consistent manifestations of the spiritual realm, the cult groups will continue to attract large numbers of baby boomers whom the Lord desires to worship Him in worship settings instead.

How to Evaluate Spiritual Experiences

Since I've never been one who enjoys being out of control, it was comforting to me to discover that I could experience the spiritual realm, and yet be in utter control of my faculties. I believe this is the apostle Paul's point when he states: "The spirits of prophets are subject to the control of prophets" (1 Cor. 14:32, paraphrased).

As we continue to see people come to us out of this spiritually sensitized culture, we began to realize that guidelines were necessary so people could evaluate the kinds of experiences and manifestations they had had or claimed to have had in the Lord. We knew God-given wisdom and discernment in this area is vital, because Satan is the arch-deceiver (see Rev. 20:2-3), and His ability to counterfeit legitimate Christian experience is well-known.

The Bible is strong and clear on how to test the veracity of our spiritual experiences. We've found it necessary, along with an atmosphere friendly to spiritual experiences, to evaluate them or help them to be maintained biblically.

Churches who attract large numbers of baby boomers will, by the very nature of our culture, be thrust into the realm of spiritual manifestations that may or may not be of God. Being able to set standards that establish (1) how spiritual gifts will be accepted in the local church and (2) how to teach and train people to test their gifts for themselves have proven to be quite valuable.

The following is a checklist we work through when sharing with those who feel they have had an experience in the Lord:

- Has experiencing this spiritual gift or manifestation taken your will from you? If so, it is not from God. *1 Corinthians 14:1-5.*
- Is it peaceful? Is this phenomenon palatable and intelligible to other spiritual people? If not, it may not be authentic. *James 3:13-18.*
- Has this occurrence glorified God? Is Jesus the center of your experience, or are you the center? It is very clear from the Bible that Jesus expected that manifestations of the spiritual realm, as authorized by Him, would always keep Him at the center. All biblically sound spiritual occurrences are Christ-centered. *1 Corinthians 12:1-3; John 14-16.*
- Did this experience cause you to be respectful of others, or did it cause you to feel superior? If it caused you to feel spiritually above others, it was

not an honest, legitimate manifestation. *1 Corinthians 14:1-5.*

- Are you willing to submit the expression of your experience to the scrutiny of your pastor and church leaders? If not, your experience would be suspect. *1 Corinthians 14.*
- Has this manifestation or insight strengthened your commitment to Christ, His Church and the foundational truths of orthodox Christianity? No legitimate experience or gift will take you to the extremes nor violate basic doctrine. *Deuteronomy 18:9-22.*
- Has this experience caused you to be more concerned about others? If so, this experience is producing the kind of fruit that is biblical and legitimate. *1 Corinthians 12-14.*
- Has this spiritual event caused you to walk in harmony with Christ? If feelings of superiority and isolation occur as a result of your experience, it may not be valid. *1 Corinthians 12.*
- Is this experience open to anyone? If you feel that it is for you only, it is probably not legitimate or genuine, for God is no respecter of persons when it comes to spiritual experiences. *Acts 10:34-36.*

This checklist is very helpful to administer to a group of people who are very highly sensitized to a viable expression and experience of their faith.

A PERSONALLY SATISFYING SPIRITUAL EXPERIENCE

We've seen in this chapter that boomers have been reared in an experience-oriented world. Our experimentation with drugs and the occult have been part of our search for reality.

For far too long, Christianity has been presented as being primarily cerebral—that is, conceived by the intellect rather than by the emotions. The boomer world, however, requires and benefits from a more all-around expression of faith—the kind of faith that involves their whole being: mind, heart and emotions and that believes God affects all their senses.

Having said that, let's get back to Bob and Betty Boomernosky and see how they're doing after their morning at church.

The service is now over. The time is 12:15 P.M. Bob is glad that the service let out on time. He is also pleasantly surprised and exhilarated by how near God seemed to be to him during the entire service.

On their way to the car, Betty comments, "I've never been around so many people who believe that God is so near. I can't wait to ask Ruth some questions on how they feel so close to Him!"

Bob opens the car door for Betty, then walks around to his door. Someone waves to him in the parking lot and he waves back, delightfully surprised by their friendliness. The kids ask to ride home with their neighbors, Randy and Ruth Boomerman.

As he slides under the steering wheel, Bob remarks: "I really enjoyed that today. I'm glad we came. How about you?"

Betty replies, "Yes, I am. The whole experience was great!"

As they pull out of the church parking lot, Betty asks, "Did you notice the number of women in leadership here? I noticed that this church even has women listed as volunteer pastors and leaders."

Though Bob hadn't noticed this, Betty had. As he muses about this while driving down the road, it also makes him feel that they had made a good choice of churches that morning.

In this next chapter, let's talk about the boomer church and women.

Notes

1. George Gallup, *Emerging Trends* (Princeton, NJ: Princeton Religion Research Center, 1988), vol. 10, no. 8.
2. Ibid.

9
WOMEN IN CHURCH LEADERSHIP

"So God created man in his own image, in the image of God he created him; male and female he created them."
—Genesis 1:27

"Prejudice is the 'Iron Curtain' of the mind."
—Anonymous

Because we boomers expect to see women in leadership, the treatment of women by the Church is a very important concern to us. Even the majority of baby boomer men desire to see women treated as equals in the Church, as well as in business.

FOR MEN ONLY?

Yet the typical, unchurched boomer assumes that the formal Church is so male-oriented that it is closed to women functioning in any capacity equal with men. This assessment saddens me, because it is generally true. The entire church culture of America still has so much inertia and reluctance to release women to preach and lead.

Somehow, the windows of opportunity need to be kicked open further for women in this decade. For, to date, a woman has had to employ near-heroic efforts to step into any area of equal expression with men in the Church.

And the irony of this situation is that, although women have never had a greater liberator than Jesus Christ and should be freer in the Church than any other place to contribute their leadership abilities, the Church has never really permitted this natural resource to be utilized.

For that reason, many boomer women fear the Church. They feel that the Church is a male-dominated club and one of the greatest enemies of their personal liberty.

While a male-oriented church used to be acceptable, it isn't anymore. So, if you don't have women in leadership, we boomers will not only think your church is out-of-date, we will also assume you are somewhat immoral. That's right—immoral!

Why? Because—when the thirty something crowd gathers in your church—even though we may not verbalize our feelings, we will note that no women are leading, evaluate church leadership behavior accordingly and conclude that such a church is bigoted!

If we enter a church where women are openly and strongly involved in all facets of church life, a positive, subliminal message about that church will be evident: This church truly represents the whole Body of Christ.

WOMEN IN MINISTRY AND LEADERSHIP

On the other hand, if we enter a church where women are openly and strongly involved in all facets of church life, a positive, subliminal message about that church will be evident, stating loudly and clearly: *This church truly represents the whole Body of Christ.* We feel deeply that communicating the gospel in a culturally intelligible way includes releasing women for substantive leadership roles in the Church.

Yet the need to release women to participate in this area is not simply cultural either. It is pragmatically impractical to fulfill our commission to propagate the gospel to the entire world, unless the Church is willing to bear its share of the task. And how can it, if leadership is denied to a greater part of the Church?

I once heard Paul Yonggi Cho, the pastor of the world's largest church, located in Seoul, Korea, say, "Until the American Church learns to release women in ministry in vast numbers, she will never see revival as we have in Korea."

I've spoken at enough pastors' conferences to know that the role of women in the Church today is essentially *the* topic of many traditions. I won't take time or space here to defend my own viewpoint exegetically. But I do underscore this witness of Scripture: *The unique reality of our Lord Jesus Christ is that, during His earthly ministry, He refused to allow dogma or the biased religious viewpoints of that era to mar the human perspective of ministry.*

Contrary to the customs of His day, Jesus freely and readily included women in the ranks of His disciples. In fact, His most trusted followers and backers often included large numbers of women. Why should it be any different today?

TAKING THE FIRST STEP

Several years ago I decided we would have to make some conscious, meaningful attempts to include women in leadership roles in our congregation. I already knew that capable women of my generation were not going to stand by and be limited in their degree of participation.

Our own journey, as a congregation, to release, train and include women in leadership roles has not been an easy one nor without hitches, however. We still have to consciously strategize our encouragement and development of women in leadership, even though we've aggressively pursued the training and releasing of women for more than five years.

I remember the night I first mentioned a strategy I felt we ought to initiate and adhere to for utilizing women's leadership capabilities in our church. As is often the case, our council meeting was running late, and we still had several more items on our agenda to discuss. But no one seemed to mind staying longer.

It was a chilly, stormy Sunday night, and we could see the rain pouring down outside, as rain can do only in Seattle in winter months. So none of us relished the idea of stepping outside at the meeting's end. After all, the warm meeting room indoors was far more inviting than the outdoors with the wind howling through the trees and the rain pelting the windows of our church office.

I paused, suggested we take a break and then announced, "We have three other items on tonight's agenda. Should we finish them all tonight or leave them until our next meeting?"

Before anyone else could reply, Chuck chimed in: "No, let's get the business over with. I'd just as soon stay 45 minutes extra this month as next."

We all agreed. After enjoying a short break, we continued the meeting.

I reconvened the meeting. "Okay, the next item on our agenda is to elect new council members. But this year, I'd like to make certain we nominate several women candidates to fill the three vacated council seats."

By their surprised expressions, I could tell that they were not prepared for this new development. For a moment, stunned silence followed as each councilman grappled with his feelings. I waited for the dust to settle.

Tom spoke first. "Doug, I've read through the material. Are you sure women will want to be part of our meetings?"

It was my turn to be surprised. After all, his wife, Joanne, is a strong individual and heavily involved in our church. They had been married for 18 years, and I had always thought Tom was quite comfortable with Joanne expressing herself as much as possible.

Before matters got too far out of hand, I interrupted to expand my viewpoint further by posing a question. "Tom, do you think Joanne would want to be part of the council?"

Stroking his brow for a moment, he answered slowly, choosing his words carefully, "Well, I don't know if I would want her to be or not."

Chuck jumped in then. "I personally think this is a bad idea. I mean, I've never been part of a church where women were on the board."

Sven, always an agreeable person, leaned forward on his elbows and stated calmly, "I don't see any reason why not. I know I'd be honored if my wife were to serve on the council."

The discussion see-sawed along these two lines for some time. At times a lot of tension was felt, but, as usual a spirit of openness gradually pervaded the meeting.

However, the more we discussed it, the harder it was for me to understand why having women on the church council was a difficult issue for these men. Then I realized that those who had struggled the most against this idea had grown up in traditional church settings where women were not allowed leadership roles. Conversely, those who had met Christ in our church and represented the core of our council constituency were unanimously quite excited about this important step.

The evening closed with a somewhat reluctant, yet unanimous, consensus that we would make a conscious effort to include three women on the upcoming council ballot.

As we departed, Phil, who was in his early 30s, nudged me and stated matter-of-factly, "I don't understand what the big deal was. After all, aren't women people too?"

THE CHALLENGE FACING WOMEN

As we progress into the 1990s, acceptance is definitely getting easier for women, but they certainly haven't arrived as yet. I recently stood up at a business meeting of our church to address the reasons why we had included several women as candidates for our church council—a concept that, after eight years, has been fully accepted by our congregation.

My statement began: "I apologize that I even have to give such an explanation. Hopefully, by next year, it will be unnecessary." But as we've grown and people have transferred their membership to our church I have necessarily had to explain—more times than I am comfortable with—why it is important that qualified women be given thoughtful places in ministry.

Karen is a very attractive person in our congregation and a very successful business woman. Her husband, Rory, is finishing his schooling and they have two children. The pressure is on both of them not only to rear their children, but also to pursue very rigorous schedules.

Karen had been married before, a union which ended in divorce several years earlier. Too late, she realized she had been wrong in running off and marrying at the age of 18 without her parents' support. Yet, even though Karen knew her first marriage was a mistake almost as soon as it began, she ended up with two children in two years.

Then with her first husband slipping into alcoholism and subjecting her to physical abuse, she wisely decided to escape that marriage. Divorce seemed the only reasonable solution for her volatile situation; yet, it was not without a great deal of pain.

About five years after that divorce, Karen gave her life to Jesus Christ. And being quite adept at public speaking, she had already begun a significant leadership role in our congregation prior to her marrying Rory. Rory's skills, on the other hand, did not include public communication, but his character and relationship with Christ were exemplary.

As Rory put it, "I just don't feel comfortable speaking. I'm just not a talker, Doug. I'm a doer. Now, as for Karen, I always agree with everything she does and says in public. In fact, I would usually say it just the way she does."

After one of our morning services, I noticed Karen strolling toward the front of the sanctuary. She obviously wanted to speak with me. As I slipped away from a group of people I'd been conversing with and extended my hand to shake hers, she spoke. "Pastor, I need to talk to you. I have mixed emotions about serving here any longer."

When she noticed my surprised expression, she quickly added, "Pastor, you just don't understand. I don't want to put Rory in the position where people think he's dominated by me in any way. So, I think it would be best if I backed off publicly as regards my contribution to this church."

I was stunned by her announcement. I really hoped that she had simply misunderstood people's reactions. But deep down, I knew there was some truth to what she said.

Out of the corner of my eye, I caught Rory standing about halfway down the aisle and motioned to him to join our conversation.

Turning back to Karen, I said, "Karen, you can do whatever you want to do in this church. No one is required, in any way, to fulfill any expectations I might have for them. I think it would be very sad, however, if you did not use your gifts to contribute to our church life here. Just think of all the people you've touched and all the people who need to be touched by your unique experiences."

Then turning to Rory as he joined our conversation, I asked, "Rory, do you feel threatened in any way by Karen's public presentations?"

Rory's quick response was, "No. I think she's just being hypersensitive."

Mildly irritated by his comment, Karen interrupted us. "No, I'm not imagining it, and I'm not being hypersensitive! I simply think it's difficult for people to perceive me as someone who is sound and sane. Besides, I'm divorced and remarried. I know this troubles many people."

It was my turn to break in. "Karen, have people said anything to you about that? If so, they're totally out of line, and I'll need to speak to them."

Karen smiled as she replied: "No, Doug, that isn't it. I appreciate your support, but people haven't said anything to me. I just know how it is."

I took a deep breath and ran my hand through my hair. I wanted to resolve this situation so I could be home to enjoy a nice Sunday lunch. I hurt for Karen though. Here was an intelligent woman, spiritually mature and capable of gifted leadership, but our culture was beginning to box her into a corner.

"Karen, you know how well we worked through the divorce issue with you. You were right to get that divorce, and Rory is a great husband. I don't think there's a person in this church who would expect you to stay in a life-threatening situation.

"Anyway, it happened a long time before you met Christ, so how can you even bring it up now? The quality of the relationship between Rory and you is evidence of your true character. You're an outstanding couple."

For a few moments neither of them spoke. Then they glanced at each other with a smile of relief. As they gripped one another's hands, I felt that the Lord had had a distinct purpose in this conversation taking place.

In a way that only He can bring about, the Lord, at that moment, spoke volumes to me in milliseconds. Condensed to just a few words, what I felt Him say to me was, *"There are many women inhibited by biases in My Church."* I felt the Lord say also that His heart ached because His Church was incomplete without their [women's] expression. And I felt Him encourage me to be even more aggressive in making sure that the Karens of the Church world would be released to serve *and* to lead in the full giftedness with which the Lord had endowed them.

When the Lord finished revealing all this to me, I concluded my conversation with Karen and Rory by saying, "Karen, at some point, you have to go against the stream, especially when you know it's right. All I can say is that I will stand by you. You're a gifted public speaker and an insightful minister. If anyone wants to criticize or harm you in any way, she or he will have to face me, too, and I think I can be pretty tough!"

We all laughed, then joined hands and prayed for a moment. I believe we all left that conversation with a new resolve and a clear understanding that even positive changes are painful at times.

The reason I've included this short anecdote about Karen and Rory is to put a face on the issue of bias and prejudice against women in church leadership roles. Sometimes, in our stereotypical approach to ministry in church life, we forget that we are hurting real persons along the way.

However, Karen's experience is by no means singular—not in our congregation nor in any other. Our congregations are filled with many experienced, talented and intelligent women who have worked through and hurdled obstacles in life that many men would never imagine facing.

Because we boomers are so attuned to the individual, we grimace at the thought of even one woman like Karen being hurt by unjustifiable prejudices within our church ranks. Yet churches across America are filled with Karens: women with less-than-perfect backgrounds, women who find themselves in a male-dominated church and very gift-ed women who don't fit the stereotypical approach to church life—and all are anxious to be released so that their gifted ministries may benefit the Church as a whole. We boomers will hail as heroic the attempts of any church leaders to make certain that the Karens of our churches are not injured or restrained by unbiblical, built-in biases.

The example of Karen and others like her suggests that it does take effort to overcome stereotypical approaches to women in ministry. The challenge is to maintain a balanced perspective when training and releasing women into church leadership roles and avoiding the pitfalls of mere tokenism or antagonistic, rebellious responses to authority in the Church.

HOW YOUR CHURCH CAN INVOLVE WOMEN IN MINISTRY

As with everything, there must be a starting point. This usu-ally begins with attitude changes and the courage to take those small, initial steps. The following practical sugges-tions can help you and your church bring competent women into positions of leadership:

Anticipate Opposition From Traditional-thinking Members

I've been surprised that even some women object to other women preaching or having leadership positions. These women were possibly taught in traditional churches that only men should lead and teach. Accepting this kind of opposition as a reality is helpful. You can then be prepared to answer any objections that may arise in a loving, rational manner.

I've heard such a preposterous comment as "Most cults were started by women." The fact remains, however, that just as many cults have been started by men as by women. Conversely, some very healthy expressions of ministry in the Body of Christ have been started by women as well as by men.

Deal with Negative Attitudes
And Stereotypical Thinking First

Dealing consciously with myths that relate to an agenda-oriented gospel is very important. For myths about women—and they are many—need to be worked against consciously, even from the pulpit.

Along with myths are stereotypical thinking and over-generalizations about women. Some of these biased, erroneous statements that create barriers for women as a gender group are:

- Women are more spiritually sensitive.
- Women are more emotional than men.
- Women are less rational and objective than men.
- Women are more subjective.
- Women tend to be indecisive.
- Women are less interested in communicating biblical principles.

And so on. Too many churches seem to foster the belief that women, as potential leaders, are second-rate material. I believe churches who foster this erroneous belief need to go full circle in countermanding such a view.

Male pastors and church leaders should begin by working on their own attitudes, being honest with themselves when facing the fact that they're prejudiced against women—and repenting. For, it's a fact: Attitudes do precede behavior.

Making grand moves to place women in leadership positions, prior to dealing with faulty attitudes within the

---

The discovery of each other's gifts and calls to service by God can be observed only as both are under the lordship of Jesus Christ. What needs to be taught is that there's nothing unmanly about being able to learn from women!

---

churches themselves, may cause more problems. No one wants to be merely tolerated or tossed out as a sacrificial lamb to allow her church to make some point. These appointments must be sincere and genuine.

It is also helpful if pastors and church leaders express their confidence from time to time in the women they have placed in positions of ministry and leadership. The leadership team can easily create an atmosphere of respect and appreciation for these women—a viable action which they should undertake.

By and large the Church world is so far behind our society's development in allowing women their voice, that lay and professional leadership in the Church, even before running to catch up, must first make conscious efforts to eliminate chauvinism in their churches. Men and women should adapt to the will of God, regardless of past traditions and perspectives.

The discovery of each other's gifts and calls to service by God can be observed only as both are under the lordship of Jesus Christ. What needs to be taught is that *there's nothing unmanly about being able to learn from women!*

Reject Tokenism

Women are most sensitive to tokenism. Token positions will never satisfy them. Knowing this to be true, I recently apprised our congregation that we—the council and I—weren't advocating mere tokenism when we recommended several women as candidates for the council. We really feel that the Lord has gifted both men and women. As Galatians 3:28 says: *"There is neither Jew nor Greek, slave nor free, male nor female, for you are all one in Christ Jesus."*

An open attitude is tantamount to believing that the Holy Spirit is moving powerfully and efficiently through all the members of His Body, *regardless of gender!* Women, therefore, should be chosen on the basis of their calling and their giftedness. And, just as with men, the question that needs to be asked of women is: Are these persons qualified?

Create Opportunities

Obviously, creating opportunities for women is essential. And it may be advisable for your church to do as our church council once did—announce outright that you believe the Lord will help you fill certain positions with qualified women so as to correct the biases that you have.

Accurately assess your need to involve women in leadership. Then establish a plan of implementation in positions of authority. Doing so may require extreme efforts at first to open up those doors of opportunity for women along with special efforts for training them.

Due to the fact that women have been hesitant in the past to step into leadership roles, not many have had opportunity to hone their leadership skills. So initiating efforts to involve such women in leadership training may be necessary as well as deliberately recruiting women for positions of authority.

Be creative in helping women to identify their spiritual gifts. Be open to find areas of service that may not be presently expressed in your congregation. By doing so, you will find it possible to open up new and exciting channels of ministry for women.

Do realize that there is a difference between the spirit of feminism, which is antimale, and the spirit of the gospel, which is promale and profemale. At the same time, work to create a view of church life that is Christ-centered rather than patriarchal. The Scriptures reveal that Jesus was always the center of the Church.

Normally, in every church, natural leaders do rise to the top. They are invariably spotted by their faithfulness, consistent service and exemplary attitudes. But I've found that gender biases often cause us to overlook women who fulfill these criteria.

Ruthless self-analysis may be necessary in this area. A helpful question to ask yourself is: have I failed to note any woman who may be just as viable as a man for this position we're filling?

I have to admit that our own church has harbored a certain amount of gender blindness—an inability to perceive women with leadership qualifications. As a result, I've found it necessary to work with a team composed of our staff and leaders to remind us periodically that we need to be sensitive by not excluding women when considering candidates for various positions.

Due to the strong male orientation of our church culture, I'm embarrassed at how often I tend to consider men first and women only secondarily for leadership positions. But, because we've established this policy to exclude no one on the basis of gender, this team, which regularly addresses balance in our implementation of leaders, has really helped us to stay on track.

Consider developing such a team in your church that can evaluate how well you're doing in addressing biases against women and how consistently women are being considered for leadership and ministry roles. This team should include several established women leaders in your church.

Encourage Husband-and-wife Ministry Teams

Foster teaching that encourages both partners in a marriage to be involved in a ministry together. Opportunities for volunteer service will need to be oriented more and more toward husband-and-wife teams. Why? Because both husband and wife usually work today and they have a shortage of time that they can share together. So ministering together will be viewed as a positive feature by both of them.

Such sensitivity to new configurations of home life will be vital in order to release women into leadership. Our church, like other boomer congregations, has had to face the fact that 85 to 90 percent of our women work outside their homes. The lion's share of these dedicated women work full-time, a fact that hardly makes for the kind of teaching that is associated today with "traditional roles" in the Church.

Today's American life-style is attainable by only a very few on one income. Consequently, most middle-class American couples today require two incomes to maintain a decent standard of living. Though this trend may be arguably unhealthy for couples with families, it is, nevertheless, a reality and a fact that the Church won't change.

We must minister to the circumstances of those we serve and that includes those of the boomer family of the '90s, a family headed by working parents with limited time at their disposal. Not only will the boomer generation family require, for instance, new teaching models with regard to home life, but new opportunities for married partners to enjoy shared responsibilities of ministry and leadership together in a way that maximizes the stewardship of the time they have available for such service.

Celebrate Women in Ministry

Celebrating ministry gifts that are being expressed in your church is a way of saying, "We have confidence in the Holy Spirit's gifting abilities as expressed through persons in this church."

In particular, make it a regular practice to celebrate women in volunteer ministries in your church in a Sunday service setting. Without making people feel conspicuous, make appropriate, positive, public statements along the lines of: "As outlined in the Bible, we welcome women to express their gifts of leadership in this church."

For the last several years, we have been rewarding our volunteer ministries in this fashion. On a Sunday morning we hand out plaques describing the various ministries which individual women have been carrying out in our church. This has been just one way we have shared our confidence not only in women, but in the total lay ministry force in our church.

That many of the lay pastors and leaders whom we acknowledge in our church happen to be women is quite incidental. This staff mix in itself offers an opportunity to celebrate the fact that we are consciously making an attempt to allow the Holy Spirit to be expressed throughout His entire Church, whether it is through men or women!

Explore What Others Say About Women in Ministry

I have included here a contemporary bibliography of authors who have written entire books, covering the theological question of women having leading roles in churches. I heartily recommend these books dealing with the issue of women in ministry in the Church. I think you will find them interesting and provocative.

Cook, Barbara E. *Ordinary Women—Extraordinary Strength: A Biblical Perspective of Feminine Potential*. Lynnwood, WA: Aglow International Publications, 1988.

Evans, Mary J. *Women in the Bible*. Downers Grove, IL: InterVarsity Press, 1983.

Foh, Susan T. *Women and the Word of God*. Phillipsburg, NJ: Presbyterian and Reformed Publishing, 1979.

Gilligan, Carol. *In a Different Voice: Psychological Theory and Women's Development*. Cambridge, MA: Harvard University Press, 1982.

Gundry, Patricia. *Neither Slave, Nor Free: Helping Women Answer the Call to Church Leadership*. New York: Harper & Row, 1987.

Martin, Faith. *Call Me Blessed: The Emerging Christian Woman*. Grand Rapids, MI: Wm. B. Eerdmans Publishing Co., 1988.

Neff, David. *Tough Questions Christians Ask.* Wheaton, IL: Victor Books, 1989.

Sayers, Dorothy L. *Are Women Human?* Grand Rapids, MI: Wm. B. Eerdmans Publishing Co., 1971.

Schussler-Fiorenza, Elizabeth. *A Feminist Theological Reconstruction of Christian Origins.* New York, NY: Crossroads Press, 1985.

Storkey, Elaine. *What's Right with Feminism?* Grand Rapids, MI: Wm. B. Eerdmans Publishing Co., 1986.

CONCLUSION

While boomer churches are slowly beginning to develop now, not only will singles represent a large segment in the Church, but churches in the 1990s will also have a number of women ordained as ministers and volunteering in the areas of leading pastoral care and teaching support for adults.

And what about the music and worship expressions in a boomer church? Is it likely that changes will be needed in the music orientation of the traditional Church? I think so.

In the next chapter, I will share some of the discoveries we have made in our own congregation that I think will be helpful across the board for all boomer churches, even though musical tastes tend to be extremely regional.

One thing is certain: The music of the late '60s to this present time has become more than a means of entertainment. It has become, more than ever, a serious means of communication. The music of the boomer world communicates throughout Western civilization a continuity in the boomer culture.

Let's discuss next how music will impact baby boomer churches.

10
ROLL OVER, CHUCK WESLEY!

I am committed to making certain that our music expresses God's predisposition to our creativity and the need to present Christianity as a journey and a pilgrimage, as well as a relevant message for all times!
—Doug Murren

COMMUNICATION AND MUSIC

Boomers communicate through music. Actually, all generations have been inclined to do this, but boomers are particularly adept at sending and receiving messages through a melody line and good rhythm.

And since music is one of the primary ways to identify with boomers, it would do every church well to examine regularly how effective its music ministry is. Is it appealing to both Christians and non-Christians? And is the quality of music offered up to par?

CONTEMPORANEITY AND MUSIC

Unchurched baby boomers will be attracted to a church that is comfortable with their music style and has familiar sounds. In other words, they will be drawn to music with a contemporary sound.

Relax, the idea of using contemporary music as a means to express worship and outreach isn't as bold or as new as it sounds. Did you know that the music to Martin Luther's "A Mighty Fortress Is Our God" was originally a barroom tune back in the sixteenth century? Also, the great hymns of Charles Wesley were melodic reflections of the nineteenth-century music contemporaneous with his period.

Most churches I have attended have missed out on what a powerful tool contemporary music can be in a service of worship and praise. A worthwhile exercise, when thinking through your service music, would be to examine your particular community's taste in music with these questions:

- Which radio stations are excelling?
- Which songs are predominantly played?
- What styles of music are popular in your area?

Anyone can obtain this kind of information, for local ratings are available. These rating systems are called Arbitrons. If you don't know how to find them, just call any local radio station and ask them for their ratings. They will, in most instances, be happy to mail them to you. I found them to be very helpful and they have given me insights into the unchurched people in our community.

Contemporary Christian rock stations used to be effective outreach tools in the past. My feeling now, however, is that they aren't as effective as they once were. The culture of rock 'n' roll has been legitimized. It is no longer considered a rebellious phenomenon. One is likely to hear music by the Beatles or The Who or any other one-time infamous popular group, now selling tennis shoes and tennis rackets.

Many dentist offices and shopping malls now play rock music from the 1960s and 1970s with no concern that it offends anyone. Why is this so? Because rock 'n' roll is the music of the predominant majority of the boomer population.

Culture and Music

If you take time to study the impact of music on our culture, you will find that the music of the baby boomer generation is likely to dominate the culture of our society well into the next century. Even our children are very comfortable with our musical tastes and identify easily with them. This identification with boomer music is likely to be the case for several more decades.

Because our particular philosophy of ministry contends that worship must be inclusive and intelligible to the baby boomer culture, we are quite comfortable with including rock-type music in our morning worship.

When it comes to us boomers, churches need to consider seriously how important a philosophy of ministry is in a total approach to church life. Developing such a philosophy of ministry is a vital first step.

Occasionally, a well-meaning Christian will ask: "Don't you think rock 'n' roll music breeds rebellion?"

I usually answer, "Rebellion against what? We baby boomers aren't rebelling against our parents anymore. And, with 76 million strong, we are now the dominant culture."

MUSIC IN A CHURCH PHILOSOPHY OF MINISTRY

Develop Your Philosophy

I have found very few churches generally that have developed any philosophy of ministry—a definition of what they consider their ministry to be and a description of how they approach it. Yet when it comes to us boomers, churches need to consider seriously how important a philosophy of ministry is in a total approach to church life. Developing such a philosophy of ministry is a vital first step.

For instance, our own church's mission statement reads in part: "Eastside Church, a local congregation, is committed to reach out to the Greater Seattle Area through an environment of love, acceptance and forgiveness."

Define Your Target Audience

Next, define your target audience. I often get caustic stares when I mention "target audience." I suppose it does sound somewhat marketing-oriented. But the point does come across: Whom are you aiming to reach?

After all, if you don't know whom God has called you to reach, how can you possibly establish a strategy for reaching them? Clearly defining your target group, therefore, is not only essential to your philosophy of ministry, but also vital in ensuring your effectiveness as a successful pastor in a greatly unchurched culture.

At Eastside Church, our primary target—that segment of the population we are particularly interested in reaching— is boomers who are, what I call, "nominal Christians." Our secondary target is the totally unchurched.

We define the "nominal Christians" in our community as "those who claim to be born again, but are not committed to any church." We believe this group may comprise as much as a third of this area's residents, with 95 percent of the people in our area being totally unchurched. Most of the people in both these groups are baby boomers like myself.

Determine Your Approach to Music

Even those churches that have developed a philosophy of ministry and have defined their target audience often have not outlined how they plan to incorporate their music and worship into their overall philosophy. Yet they need to do so, for music is such a large part of the life of any church, and it should reflect the specific call of its congregation and agree with its philosophy.

How we approach our music has been a vital part of the development of our philosophy of ministry at Eastside Church. All our music has a specific outreach theme. And all music in our congregation:

- must be culturally relevant,
- must be comparable in quality and excellence with what our target groups are listening to,
- must communicate our values, and
- must enhance the atmosphere of worship.

These are tall orders to fill in any music program. But once we know what our aim is, it is possible to do it.

THE MINISTRY OF MUSIC

Our worship is not only associated with rock 'n' roll music, but we will often take the tune of a popular hit from the last 20 years—which many people will recognize—and rewrite the lyrics that go with it.

Phil (not his real name), a great friend of mine in our congregation, was once a concert promoter of rock 'n' roll groups in the 1960s. Though he is now the middle-aged father of three college students, he still loves rock 'n' roll. He is also a committed Christian, a valued participant in our church and a very successful businessman.

Recently, Phil and I were discussing the music in our services.

"Hey, Phil, how do you like our music lately?" I asked.

Phil has told me that he takes the music part of our worship very seriously because he works in the conservative business world. Knowing his background, I also knew he would probably give me a balanced perspective.

As Phil replied, enthusiasm was evident in his voice. "You know that song the soloist did three weeks ago? Paul Simon's "Bridge Over Troubled Water"?

"Yeah, Phil, it was great, wasn't it?"

"It sure was, Doug. You know, that same week, I was really under the gun. As I was driving down the freeway one day that week, that same tune came on the radio. I didn't realize you had changed much of the lyrics until I found myself singing our Christian adaptation.

"Now I know why you do that. What a surge of life filled my spirit! Christ filled my world, right in the middle of that freeway! I felt the inspiration of the service all over again. Way to go. Keep it up, Doug!"

Phil had confirmed my strategy. I felt that if we could take a familiar tune every several weeks and write some new, Christian lyrics for it, we would be able to communicate the gospel in the middle of our culture. I truly believe the life of Jesus Christ wants to invade the daily lives of those I love and serve. And I strongly believe that music and ministry through music are a vital part of that communication.

Other pastors ask me from time to time how I know when our worship music is on target. I tell them that one of the primary ways I know is when—after a service—the young folk all tell me they enjoyed the music and the older worshippers all tell me they didn't. Then I feel quite certain that we are probably on target for the unchurched baby boomers who attend.

I realize that other groups, who would be targeted indirectly by or to baby boomers, may have very different

approaches to a philosophy of ministry as well as to music.
I can say only that our music philosophy is aimed directly
at this group, which underlies the primary focus of our particular church.

Actually, an eight-point checklist guides us in developing the style of music we use. These important eight points
form the premises undergirding the strategy we have chosen and developed for music in our worship services:

1. We believe music—scores, as opposed to lyrics—is
   amoral (neither moral nor immoral).
2. We believe music is a communicative tool and
   device for evangelism and outreach.
3. We believe music is one of the clearest and most
   profound forms of worship expressions our human
   spirit can offer to God, who deserves the best, not
   mediocrity.
4. We believe every human being was created to worship God and hungers to do so. Truly heartfelt worship is in itself not only an expression of evangelism, but also of healing to our human spirit.
5. We believe music is a viable tool to instruct and to
   allow our human spirit an opportunity to experience God's divine touch.
6. We believe music in church should be of a quality
   and style comparable to that of the culture-at-large.
7. We believe music in church shouldn't be very much
   different from the music that fills our everyday lives
   in order for it to communicate effectively.
8. We believe music should be the balance of a verti-
   cal, God-related focus and a horizontal ministry of
   comfort, exhortation and evangelism. This balance
   must be maintained seriously if the worship,
   through musical experience, is to be fruitful.

THINKING ABOUT WORSHIP

What is worship? Worship is an expression of devotion that involves the whole person. Worship is a 24-hour, seven-days-a-week calling for Christians.

I believe that worship is not primarily about us; *worship is absolutely about God.*

When I look at our worship services, I am very concerned that the whole person be affected. I'm also concerned that our worship will have even more impact beyond our services. Our worship services involve only a portion of a believer's expression of praise throughout their entire week, but they ought to enhance and strengthen our worship through our labor, relationships, family life and devotional life.

Yet, if we don't understand what we're doing, it isn't truly worship. Just as the Chinese aren't expected to worship God in English, neither should boomers be required to worship God in forms unintelligible to them. They require a unique approach to worship.

I'm hopeful, as I think about our worship services every Sunday, that our worship in music and song will accomplish four things. Our weekly self-analysis evaluates how well these four things happened:

1. Did the songs invite our hearts to experience the "now" presence of God?
2. Did the preaching and teaching help us to grow in right thinking about God (that is, in worship)?
3. Was our prayer life enhanced by an increase in our faith? Did we feel that we truly communicated our heartfelt response to God?

4. Did our worship experience create a more powerful and renewed vision of His presence filling our
entire life?

WORSHIP IS OUTREACH

Likewise, worship can be an outreach. I truly believe that,
in our time, worship must be considered as an integral part
of our outreach. Because I believe our human hearts
hunger to worship God, I also believe that even an
unchurched person can be involved in a worship experience during their first-time gathering with Christians.

But clear thinking about worship that is effective to
Christian growth and outreach is important. Though a very
difficult balance to maintain, it must be aimed at, nevertheless.

In evaluating our worship as an outreach tool, our music
team gathers together each week to evaluate what choruses
we plan to sing, what special music to be performed and
how that music will interface with the message for that
week. Such evaluations are based on the following criteria:

Is Our Worship Inclusive?

Because I believe worship is a strong outreach tool, I desire
that both the first-time visitor and the utterly unchurched
will be able to participate in our worship. I've noted that
much of Christianity has very esoteric worship music in
which visitors are usually unable to participate.

For even the first-timer to be able to participate in the
musical expression of praise in a worship service, this
involves an evaluation of the lyrics to be sung.

- Are the lyrics simple enough so that first-time visitors can join in?

- Are the lyrics available in such a form that a first-time participant can be part of the worship experience?

If a congregation expects a large number of unchurched people to visit their sanctuary, they must always be mindful of and be prepared for people who do not know the lyrics of the songs to be sung.

What is worship? Worship is an expression of devotion that involves the whole person. Worship is a 24-hour, seven-days-a-week calling for Christians. I believe that worship is not primarily about us; worship is absolutely about God.

Because our tradition has always been strong for free, spontaneous worship, I am at times asked by one of our music team, "Why was our worship off today?"

My simple response is "Because we had so many visitors who didn't know the songs."

Over time, we've learned that if our worship is to be inclusive of visitors, it must be contemporary enough for them to be comfortable. The lyrics must be readily available for people to be included. You can do this also by having your own numbered songbook, by including a sheet in your bulletins—if you use them—with the choruses for that Sunday typed or printed on them, or by using an overhead projector—if funds allow.

We have accomplished both of these—having both contemporary worship and readily available lyrics—by adjusting our presentation and style of musical arrangements. We have also placed a large-vision screen in our sanctuary where we display the lyrics of our choruses and hymns.

In addition, when I read the Bible text for the day, it is also displayed on this screen, along with the points in the message. This helps those who have not brought a Bible to be included in the worship of the Word as well. Everyone in our sanctuary is then able to participate, whether they've been here eight years or one day.

Is Our Worship Participative?

Freedom to participate is a vital element in worshiping outreach. Baby boomers want to participate, not just spectate. Participative worship is that which includes everyone in the sanctuary in such a way that their whole being becomes involved. In our particular format we often join hands together when we pray. I believe this allows for a sense of participation and togetherness in our prayer times.

The method used by a worship leader should aim at making everyone feel as if they are participating in something. The comments we make during services are made to involve and include everyone present in our fellowship. We discuss every element in our services as an opportunity to join in. This aspect is very, very important. As people participate in the activity of worshiping, they become better worshipers.

We are disinclined to have special, professional singers perform in our church. We would rather have those with this particular gift and calling, who are also regular participants in our church, minister music to our congregation. When the congregation sees people in their midst who have worked hard to train and prepare for a ministry in music, I believe they feel as though they are participating right along with them.

Is Our Worship Truly Representative Of Those Whom I Lead?

We have many professional singers call us who do want to sing at our services. However, we accept only a few, our reason being that the vast majority of these professional singers are from more traditional approaches to worship, which generally don't fit in with our approach.

As stated earlier, I am really not concerned about attracting people already churched to our church. Transfer growth, in my mind, is not desirable growth. I'm aiming to pastor those people in my community who are unchurched.

I was recently asked about the size of our congregation.

Because one of our primary motivations is evangelism, I replied, "Approximately 700,000 people." This figure, of course, represents those people within 20 to 30 minutes of our church site.

At first, the person laughed, thinking I was kidding around, then realized that I was serious. I've repeatedly stated to our congregation that when people become believers and disciples in our church, they are called to help me pastor a community which is mostly unchurched and greatly in need of Christ's touch.

I frequently ask myself: *Is the music and worship time in our church services truly representative of the tastes and style of the people whom I'm called to lead?*

Have We Kept a Balance of Worship
And Ministry in Our Special Music?

This factor is something that can't necessarily be evaluated from week to week. I look at this matter over a continuum because it allows me four to six weeks to evaluate where we've been musically and where we're headed. This review and evaluation, I believe, is one of my primary roles as a pastor.

I must evaluate the songs for their content and quality. I must not only be aware of a wide variety of innovative styles and forms that are intelligible to those to whom we are ministering, but also examine whether our music is fulfilling our philosophy of ministry and aims.

I regularly evaluate songs as to whether the musicians on our behalf involve us in worship to God and whether the musicians are speaking on God's behalf to us. I really believe that an absolute balance is essential in this kind of music.

If there is too much exhortative, admonitional or comforting music from God to man, I believe it lends itself to a high degree of performance-oriented worship. On the other hand, music that does not involve a sense of God's flow of life and ministry to His people develops at some point a distancing between worshipers and Christ.

So, on Wednesday morning, I evaluate the previous Sunday services, as well as the upcoming services, by asking myself: *How are we doing on this continuum?* Our musicians have learned well how to work with this balance.

Worship and Tradition

Tradition is a good thing. It is *traditionalism* that is the enemy of the gospel. The Church has centuries of valuable traditions of which each congregation should take advantage.

In our quest for innovative ministry, I am concerned that our congregation not leave behind the healthy aspects of tradition. It is for this reason that we sing one hymn each Sunday, for which we usually create a contemporary arrangement that remains true to the original.

This has proved to be a wonderful way to link up with the rich heritage of the Christian Church. I believe this is one of the primary ways in which we can tie ourselves to church traditions and history, but release ourselves into the awesome sovereignty of God as well. Worship, ultimately, ought to leave all who walk out of a church awe-inspired with how big, how great God is. There is nothing like the traditional hymns to allow our human hearts to experience this reality.

Musical Outreach Events

I've read a number of polls, surveys and figures as to why people attend church. It's my feeling that about half the people polled would come to a special event if they were invited. In other words, many more people are likely to come to a special event than to a church service as their first exposure to any congregation.

Our church now performs at least two musical outreaches a year. We got this idea just before we moved into our new building in 1989. Initially, we wanted to give our creative people opportunities to use their crafts and skills to touch others with the message of Christ through music.

But we soon realized that this was one of the most viable, effective outreach devices we could use in our community. We sell tickets to these events at very low prices, which rarely cover even our expenses. And we have these special events at times other than Christmas or Easter, as people tend to come at these times anyway.

After we started presenting these musicals, I learned that several churches in other areas of America have also done them effectively and found them well received. Willow Creek Community Church in South Barrington, Illinois, pastored by Bill Hybels, has some of the most powerful and effective musical outreaches in the country.

We have found that nearly half of unchurched people will come to a high-quality event that is intelligible to them. I usually take a few weeks to encourage and train people on how to share this opportunity with their friends, neighbors and relatives. And the response has been overwhelming, so much so that we rarely advertise these events outside our church, for they're usually sold out by folks in our own congregation.

These musical events have drawn hundreds to give their lives to Christ and have convinced us that music is one of the most powerful tools available to the church for reaching baby boomers. When someone in our church brings a friend to an event and that person meets Christ because of that event, he or she is assimilated into our church right away. That's why this kind of outreach is used best in the hands of local churches.

Christian performers are great, but our congregation "owns" these events with intense devotion, and they "own" them far more when they come to watch performances by our own gifted people than if they come to watch professional Christian performers at work, great though they may be.

When people attend our musical events, they are usually quite surprised that the music isn't all religious. Though the message is always poignant, the music is designed to allow hearts to feel "at home" with the culture of our times as they hear the message of the gospel. In putting together one of our musical events, we take contemporary songs from the 1960s through the 1980s and theme them to a script. Professional directors, musicians and writers then take our team's ideas and put them to work for us.

A humorous, but favorable comment about our church came from a visitor who had attended one of our recent musical performances after being invited by one of our regular worshipers. Sharon (not her real name) has been part of our church for several years and had brought three co-workers from her office to this particular musical.

One day, as I was about to leave after a service, Sharon excitedly grabbed my arm. "Pastor, don't slip out too quickly. I want to tell you what happened at the last musical."

"Sure thing, Sharon. Tell me what happened. I'm all ears."

"Well, I brought three people from work. One of them, Larry [not his real name], had been terribly antagonistic toward the gospel. He's a highly moral man, however, is in his mid-40s and loves his kids, but said he's always hated church. Well, after he came to our musical the other night, he left ecstatic!"

"Wow! That's really exciting, Sharon. I'm glad you brought that many people. Tell me. Did he commit his life to Christ?"

"No, not yet, Doug, but he's going from desk to desk in our office—we have approximately 200 employees—and telling them how great my church is! And that they wouldn't believe the music we have and how unreligious we are!

"Doug, here's what's exciting. This guy was considered by all the Christians in my office to be a hopeless case. But I actually heard him say to one of our employees that if he were ever to go to church, he'd go to my church, because we talk his language."

The Element of Shock

Because boomers really expect church music to be dull, they are totally caught off-guard when a church performs music well. That puts the element of surprise in our favor each week and opens the door for a strong, powerful ministry. Actually, any church that will put forth any kind of effort will enhance its music and will be rewarded—as will be those who hear it—with surprising results.

Sophisticated Listeners

Churches, as a whole, overlook the fact that the concerts we boomers generally attend and the music we listen to are directed and orchestrated by those who spend millions to obtain a high quality of sound. So when it comes to sound quality, boomers are very sophisticated. And we are no less demanding when it comes to the quality of musicianship.

Most boomers now have stereo systems that were unimaginable even 20 years ago. In fact, our entire culture has become fanatically sound sensitive. For about $800, a stereo system can be purchased today that has better sound than the equipment used in the production of *Sgt. Pepper's Lonely Hearts Club Band* a mere two decades ago.

Perhaps you've seen the Maxell Tape Company's ad in *Time* or *Newsweek.* Maxell makes cassette tapes. The subheading under their ad reads, "Experience the sound." The photo shows a thirty something man listening to his small speakers that are so powerful that his hair and muffler are being blown backwards.

So just by improving their sound system or their instrumentation, churches can vastly increase their potential for reaching boomers. Yet one of the mistakes made repeatedly by churches is trying to make do with inferior sound systems that are equipped with little more than treble and bass knobs. Why? Because most church leaders give very little thought to lighting or sound. Hence, the listening and viewing environment is far less than satisfactory.

One of my pet peeves is that many congregations fail to address how terrible most of their church sound systems are. So at seminars I like to tell pastors, "It's okay to have hard chairs, but please have good sound. Go without carpeting if you have to, but do have good music. You don't need bulletins, but you do need to buy the best instruments you can afford.

"Good sound and production excellence will attract large numbers of potential boomer members to your church in any city. Unchurched baby boomers are actually offended and turned off when the quality of the sound system and musicianship are substandard. So if your church will put good money into these systems, you will increase tenfold the interest of boomers in your messages."

The Cost

Okay, we're talking sound systems. So what kind of costs are we looking at? You'll get a good idea, if you sit in on one of our church staff meetings.

Seven of us met together—two from our pastoral staff, three from our building committee and two architects—to discuss the final phases of our building plans. After we gulped down decaffeinated coffee and cookies, we unfolded the plans for our new facility. We had decided that Phase I would provide seating for 1,400 people.

Though our budget was now limited after we'd purchased 20 acres, we all believed that our dream could be accomplished in a multiphase approach to construction. Our architect checked through the project's cost for land and development. Then he moved to the cost of footings and on through the overall construction of the building.

Everyone nodded in agreement as the various costs were rattled off, for the prices appeared to be in order. We also decided on the woman who would handle the interior design. When these decisions were disposed of, the architect leaned forward and announced, "Now, we come to the sound system. Gentlemen, this is where we have a problem."

I could see faces stiffen as I looked around the room. Everyone glanced in my direction. I was definitely on the spot.

The architect, who was used to building conventional churches, was having difficulty understanding why I wanted to spend so much on lighting and sound. When we had met with the Council and had talked about this before, I had apprised them that we would be spending a large sum on our sound system, and would be instituting a phase process for upgrading our lighting capacity on a yearly basis.

The architect continued, "Pastor, according to the sound engineer, the cost will be quite a bit higher than we'd hoped."

John, who was always a straight shooter, turned to me and asked, "Why do we have to spend this kind of money, Doug? Nearly one-tenth of the cost of the facility is going into sound. If you figure just the hard construction, we'll be putting nearly 20 percent into sound. The last church I was in, I think we spent only $2,000 to $3,000 on the sound system."

Turning to the architect, John asked, "Is this cost a customary expense?"

Though unhappy with the comparison he had made, I knew John's heart was always in the right place. Eventually, they all ended up understanding why I wanted to go to this large expense for sound and lighting. I pulled out the architectural bid and glanced at it again. Sure enough, it would be quite an expense!

"Gentlemen," I began, "remember when we went over our priorities in our building program, as well as over some of the nonnegotiables?"

Everyone nodded in agreement.

I continued. "Okay, I guess we're beginning to discover that some of our convictions do cost money. I want to suggest, however, that if we don't put in a proper sound system, if it's hard to hear in the new sanctuary or if the sound is flat and unappealing, we'll never be able to use this new facility adequately.

"If the sound system is bad or inadequate—and sound is the largest portion of our communication—we will have wasted all this money. Our worship and music are the most vital parts of our church experience together. The sound system must work *for* us and not against us."

"Can't we add just a little at a time?" asked Dave.

Before I could respond, the architect interjected, "No, if Doug is right about this, you need to put in the best sound system you can right now."

The meeting wound down. By the time we finished, we were once again committed to our philosophy of ministry. We also became fully aware that evening that every commitment carries a cost with it—in our case, the commitment to install a quality sound system that would appeal to our target ministry group: baby boomers. This outreach meant spending whatever money was required to accomplish the desired results.

The bottom line was definitely more than we'd anticipated. However, when we recommitted ourselves to understand the people we aimed to reach—the thirty something gang—we decided to invest whatever was necessary in the sound system, believing it to be an avenue to ministry.

And our sound system has become just that. The return in souls won has more than justified the investment we made in installing a quality listening and viewing environment.

CREATIVE OPTIONS

"Pastor, why don't we have a choir in this place?" a woman in our membership meeting asked me.

I cleared my throat, because I hated to answer her question. I'm always tempted to answer that question by replying, "We don't have a choir because I frankly don't care for them."

But because I understand this feeling represents my personal prejudice, I hold it in. I also feel—and it's being confirmed—that the Lord will someday release His expression through choirs in our midst.

So, smiling broadly, I replied instead, "We don't have a choir because we view our entire congregation as a choir." Thankfully, this answer satisfied both the enquirer and everyone else in the room.

Now, I think choirs are fine, and most churches across America will continue to have them. Obviously, one of the great benefits of choir music is the possibility of involving a large number of people in this ministry.

But innovation of any kind is appreciated by baby boomers, and the innovative capacity to keep incorporating new forms of music and style in our congregation and outreach is very important.

When I spoke recently with a very popular Christian performer in America, I commented about the fact that he's now performing rap music in his concerts.

He answered, "You know, it's interesting, but the youth pastor of our church, who met Christ in one of my rock 'n' roll concerts about 20 years ago, said that rap was a rebellious form of music, and he didn't believe the Lord wanted me to use it as a means of reaching today's kids."

We both laughed. Then I reminded him of the way he had met Christ 20 years ago himself. It was through one of *our* rock concerts, and people were saying the same thing then. How quickly Christians move from a creative posture to the comfort of the predictable and the safety of the past.

I believe there really is a balance to be maintained when using innovative music. I watch very closely that we don't slide over to what I call "cute." Cute is the attempt to appear to be "hip" or contemporary. Innovativeness for the sake of innovation is not effective at all. Innovation ought to match up with the criteria and line up with a specific philosophy of ministry.

Nevertheless, with baby boomers, innovation is always appreciated. We are, by nature, adventurous in the styles and forms of music we use. *I am committed to making certain that our music expresses God's predisposition to our creativity and the need to present Christianity as a journey and a pilgrimage, as well as a relevant message for all times!*

A PRACTICAL REVIEW

Let's summarize now what we have covered in this chapter and consider as well some practical advice toward developing music that is boomer sensitive:

- Every church leader should be ruthless when analyzing his or her church's music and sound system. Poor public address systems, poorly prepared music, inferior singers, haphazard presentations and poorly designed acoustics all speak loudly to the boomer who has been brought up with a great deal of sound sophistication that this church isn't really committed to being first-rate.

At the same time, being first-rate can be expensive, so churches ought to evaluate the cost of performing good music and presenting quality sound.

- Each congregation should stand vehemently opposed to mediocrity, for one of the greatest obstacles to the unchurched is the Church's long-standing tendency to be satisfied with mediocrity— or worse. Not only will mediocrity become immediately evident to baby boomers, it is also inconsistent with the Christian message, for God deserves and should have the best that a church can afford.

- Churches, consequently, ought to involve the very best of musicians available to them. Churches that give a great deal of time and attention to improving their music ministry will receive "many happy returns."

In our early church life, we didn't have the best musicians, but we at least had them take lessons and obtain training and determined that they were the kind of people who would pursue excellence in their ministry expression. Excellence in the presentation of music is quickly recognized by boomers who will listen to almost anything if it is done well. If we have organ music, then it had better be done well.

That doesn't mean, however, that content is not important. Church life without content is like eating cereal without milk. Yet, the style and quality of music have everything to do with how well our message is being communicated to our target group.

- Every congregational leader should determine if their use of music lines up with their philosophy of ministry. Music should not be an imitation of what the church culture does at-large. Music in each congregation should be specifically aimed to the purposes and philosophy of that particular congregation.
- Leaders need to realize that rock 'n' roll is the primary communicative mode of our baby boom culture. It can be used as a very effective communication tool and ought to be used as such.
- Churches ought to evaluate the ease with which visitors can participate in worship services. Ask such questions as *Does it require special insight or experience to participate with us?* If so, visitors won't return.

Ruthless self-analysis of your services is necessary. Also ask *Are our services sensitive to visitors?*

And particularly ask *Is our music appealing to those who would join us for the first time?*

Worship is a participative experience. Great effort should be made to include and involve people in worship experiences that are nonperformance in nature, yet participative by design.

PARTICIPATIVE—AND POSITIVE

Once again, let's go back and visit our friends, Bob and Betty Boomernosky. As they relax in their living room, they discuss their new church experience with their children.

One of their kids spoke. "Mom, I really liked my class today. It was exciting."

"Yeah, me too. I thought it was going to be dull, but it was neat," echoed the other.

Bob and Betty turned to each other, pleased by this comment. Their children had actually had a positive experience with God that day.

Betty looked at Bob and remarked, "You know, there's one thing in particular I really liked about that service, Bob."

"Yeah? What was that, Betty?"

"Well, everything they had to say was so positive. I remember church as being so negative when I was a girl—you know, all about going to hell and all that kind of stuff."

"You're right. I hadn't thought about that until you mentioned it just now."

Bob folded up the paper, walked across the living room and turned on the tube to watch the afternoon game.

We boomers are very suspicious of anything that sounds fundamentalistic. Our real hope, when we go to church, is that someone will say something positive and encouraging. People today live in a very negative world, so they expect—and need—church to be contrastingly positive.

Let's discuss this feature of reaching out to baby boomers in the next chapter.

11
Can't They Say Something Positive?

"The assertion that this generation is somehow special has defined the baby boom from the beginning. It is not the first generation to make this claim, but none has ever said it more force-fully or convincingly."
—Landon Jones[1]

"The tongue that brings healing is a tree of life."
—Proverbs 15:4

"A cheerful look brings joy to the heart and good news gives health to the bones."
—Proverbs 15:30

THE negativism of the times we live in has created an intense hunger for a positive message. And that is not surprising where baby boomers are concerned. Boomers have always been consummate optimists anyway—a trait we somehow missed passing on to our kids. I sometimes think that boomers will go to their graves still believing in the dream of a perfect world.

WHAT IS THE CHURCH *FOR*?

People unacquainted with our church often ask if our congregation is negative or legalistic in the way we represent the Christian faith. Why do they ask that? Because unchurched baby boomers generally have the overwhelming impression that the Church is a negative, legalistic institution. And they tend to feel that way because whatever church experiences they've had in the past have been negative and legalistic.

Even today, boomers don't find a bright outlook on life in many churches. Rather, we perceive churches generally—at least from the tone and content of their messages—as evidencing a high level of preoccupation with the horrors of hell and the terribleness of sin.

And when it comes to expressing their views of lost humanity, too many churches still echo Isaac Watts' unfortunate "such a worm as I" language in referring to themselves and others. Though unchurched boomers may privately acknowledge they are flawed—and maybe even sinful—they are hardly going to sit in a public place and listen to themselves being described as worms, wretches, fallen creatures and other totally depraved types.

On TV, too, we frequently see Christian leaders critical of this, that and the other thing. And too often it seems that Christians only get in the news when they're picketing, marching or demonstrating against something.

So what we really would like to know is: What is the Church for?

REALIZING THE CHURCH'S NEGATIVE IMAGE

Surely, few people view legalism or negativism as a healthy feature of any church. And certainly, neither is a healthy experience for the human spirit. No one senses these assertions to be true more than do baby boomers who are now returning to church. Boomers will instinctively reject any penchant toward such attitudes that they encounter. But they respond favorably when the reality of God's judgment is balanced with the positive message of God's grace and redemption in Jesus Christ.

The March 1989 issue of *Emerging Trends*, published by the Princeton Religion Research Center, highlighted the fact that reaction against religious negativism is on the rise. This newsletter reported that bias against such negativism has increased from 11 percent in 1981 to 13 percent in 1987 and to 30 percent in 1989.[2] The unchurched I encounter confirm these findings.

Churches that endeavor to reach baby boomers then will have to figure out how to be true to the orthodox faith while, at the same time, shedding the negative image they've acquired. For when it comes to religion, there has probably never been another generation as resistant to guilt motivation as boomers. As might be said in Deep South terminology, "There ain't a whole lot of fear of the Lord around these parts."

Crisis evangelism is not as effective with this group either. In ministering to the thirty something crowd, my whole approach to how believers experience holiness, as translated to each individual, has had to be readjusted.

We have discovered at Eastside Church that this generation will not be forced into prescribed notions of spirituality. And one of the reasons is that baby boomers have such a high regard for individualistic spirituality. Consequently, they will thrive in churches which allow people to progress in the Christian faith at the pace each can handle.

I think another of the reasons that church life often seems so negative to outside observers is that they themselves are really quite angry with the world. And such persons are often greatly tempted to take out their hostility toward the world on those with whom they gather to worship and learn.

But I've also observed that some Christians are no less angry about both the state of the world-at-large and their own personal world. And though they are the exception and not the rule, they too tend to take their anger out on those gathering in their midst who are searching intensely for answers. Jesus Christ's unique ability to love those hostile to Him is a trait that needs to be emulated much more by those in the Church who claim to bear His name.

THE POWER OF POSITIVE SPEECH

As a pastor to boomers, I'm convinced that they need to hear even negative messages presented in positive terms. It's the grid through which we filter things. So if we can't be positive—even when talking about negative topics—boomers will probably not listen.

We need to be very careful, therefore, about the tone we take in our services. Emotionally charged topics—such as abortion, divorce, drug use and alcoholism—all need to be handled with compassion and tact in any church that truly desires to be open to the nominally Christianized baby boomers.

That's why I am careful never to talk about any of these emotionally charged issues, unless I can take a full hour in a midweek service to discuss a particular issue thoroughly from several perspectives. I don't want anyone to misinterpret the positive message of Jesus Christ.

I've made a deliberate practice of making sure that the messages I direct to my age-group always strike a positive note. Now, I'm not backing down on the biblical premise that we are all fallen sinners and desperately need to be saved. Admittedly, we are depraved; yet the gospel also presents the premise that because we were created in God's image, God considered us of high enough value to send His Son to redeem us.

Nevertheless, for baby boomers to give listening ears, pastors somehow need to bring this message into balance. The great challenge is how to present the reality of God's judgment and the need for our transformation in such a way that boomers are won to Christ, not alienated from the Church.

DIFFERENT TIMES REQUIRE DIFFERENT MESSAGES

In times past the human spirit was far more sturdy than it is now. Modernity has taken a high toll of the human spirit, as has the high cost of the American dream. The stress of modern life has had a greatly negative impact on the self-esteem of modern man.

Consequently, there is a high level of fragility in the modern human ego. Boomers particularly have been fragmented and shattered by the fast pace of modern-day development. That's why our baby boomers today are in a very fragile state.

Have you ever taken the time to read messages by some of the great nineteenth-century preachers, such as the renowned theologian, revivalist and educator, Charles G. Finney? If you have, you will probably have noted that he—and others of his era—addressed quite a different crowd than we do today and they addressed them in a very different manner. And because of those differences, I disagree with those who say that such messages are appropriate for our time.

You see, people in our culture are truly broken and deeply wounded. They need desperately to be healed and put back together. But the process of healing, I believe, is different for every era and every generation, including this one.

Yes, different times do require different messages. Let me illustrate:

It was a beautiful fall afternoon. My old friend, Ollie (not his real name), was teaching me how he'd learned to graft different varieties of apples onto one trunk. Most of that year's apples were already picked, with some of the remaining already on the ground.

As we stepped off the porch, I stepped on several fallen apples, squashing them up around my new tennis shoes. To clean them off, I wiped my feet on the higher grass around the trees. Ollie looked at me half apologetically and said, "I always leave some for the little animals who often hang around. You have to leave a little food they like."

As we walked out to the edge of his property and started down the ravine to his lower orchard, Ollie's mood became serious. Pulling up his bib overalls and running his hand through his long, silver hair, he said, "You know, Pastor, I've been wanting to have you over to talk about all those young people down at our church. I sure love 'em, you know."

"Yes, I do too, Ollie," I replied, realizing that something of great concern to him was about to surface.

"You know, I never heard someone like you who believed the same things I do. In fact, I hold those things we believe really dear. You know, I don't know how we agree so much, but we do, though you sure sound different than I do.

"But, I don't think you talk about sinning enough, Pastor. Those kids need to be prepared to live in a pretty rough, sinful world, you know."

"So you don't think I talk enough about sin, Ollie."

I smiled and patted him on the shoulder as we walked on. I tried not to sound condescending. Ollie had proved himself to be a faithful man. He and his wife were the epitome of a strong Christian couple.

Ollie continued. "You know, rumor has it that a lot of those kids have been divorced and are sleeping around. Do you know that, Pastor? They need to hear some stern talk sometimes. I know you're reaching them. I just hope they'll be healthy Christians. You know what I mean, Pastor?"

Smiling, I replied, "Yes, Ollie, I know what you mean."

From past comments he had made, I knew Ollie's heart definitely agreed with what we were doing.

Slowly, I responded, "Ollie, do you think that different times require different messages?"

"Yep," he replied.

"Well, I think this is an interesting time we're living in. Did you ever notice that most of our congregation is the thirty something crowd?" I asked.

"You bet I noticed that. In fact, sometimes my wife and I talk about whether we even belong in this church."

"Yeah, you belong all right, Ollie," I reassured him. "In fact, you think a lot like those kids do. And times are changing awfully fast. The people we're reaching are living in a world that is pretty negative. Both the TV and the papers are filled with a lot of bad news.

"The reason we're having so much fun in our church is that these people want to be around where folks are positive. On account of all these negatives—like pollution, acid rain, overpopulation, nuclear war, cholesterol—this just doesn't seem to be a safe world anymore. So they want to hear something positive when they gather to hear the gospel.

"Actually, they *need* to hear something positive, Ollie. You see, I want their ear. It's kind of like your apples here on the ground. You leave a few because you know that's what the little animals like. You leave them so they'll come back around.

"Well, we in the church need to leave a few tidbits around too so that folks will come back. They're also hungry for something positive."

HOW TO BE HEARD WITHOUT COMPROMISING

On another occasion, I had flown into Los Angeles to meet with other pastors and church consultants of varied backgrounds in a conference on the nature of the unchurched in our time. Some of those present were young and some were old, but all intensely interested in the unchurched.

The meeting went on all day with much free exchange of information and opinion. Then, in the afternoon, during the final portion of our meeting, the discussion turned to the lack of conviction of sin evident in some of the larger, growing churches in America. This isn't a thesis that I've held to myself as I've been around the church world long enough to know that no one is doing very well in the sinless category.

One pastor commented, "What concerns me is that some of these larger, faster-growing churches are catering to a cul-

---

I hope that we can trust the Holy Spirit enough that we can encourage an environment in which the turned-off and the burned-out can respond to the gospel, and that...hearts will receive the healing they so desperately need.

---

ture, rather than challenging this culture." The atmosphere became only mildly tense over that remark, for most of us attending were used to such statements at these meetings.

Someone else jumped in. "Well, maybe in a time of heightened evangelism our churches are filled with more people who are in the process of moving toward conversion."

This observation was my cue to add my two-bits worth: "I believe that's true. We'll have transitional people in the 1990s—people who are going to churches that identify with their language. They're hearing something in those churches that strikes a chord in their hearts."

One of my pastor friends from the Midwest added: "I think it's probably true that we're living in a missionary time. And though I dislike the worn-out term, 'Post-Christian Era,' we really are living in such a period. I think some of the reasons the more positive gospel-oriented groups are growing is that people do need to hear a positive message."

The discussion then turned from that topic to another. I mention this dialogue and refer to the tension it generated only to accentuate the fact that the tension between missionary sensitivity and gospel character is always felt more keenly in a time of great growth in any church.

When the meeting ended, I prayed that those of us who are gravely concerned about the unchurched would not compromise the gospel as my pastor colleague feared. And this is a legitimate concern.

However, I hope that we're intelligent enough and trust the Holy Spirit enough that we can permit and encourage an environment in which the uninitiated, the turned-off and the burned-out can respond to the gospel, and that churches will present the gospel in such a way that hearts will receive the healing that they so desperately need.

That afternoon exhausted me, and I've continued to carry the awareness of that unresolved issue that we grappled with that afternoon. It's an issue that won't disappear easily. In fact, it may be one of the greater conflicts that churches will face in the 1990s—*how to be heard without compromising.*

ARE WE POSITIVE? YES! ARE WE COMPROMISED? NO!

One afternoon in 1986, I was reviewing our strategy for the upcoming year. We had had an extraordinary year of growth, mostly those folks in the thirty something range. I was astounded by how much we had grown. I knew of a number of other churches who were also experiencing similar growth in the same audience we were attempting to reach.

A number of people in our congregation have left cults. And a variety of groups began coming to us seeking for help. Sometimes it would be an influx of older people. Other times we'd have runs on drug addicts. It seemed as though people of different types and sizes came to our church in streams that year.

I was sitting in a house that we'd converted into offices across the street from our sanctuary. It was a hot summer afternoon, and I was thankful that the former bedroom I was using as my office was shaded by a large willow tree. As I thumbed through the demographics and charts of our statistical growth that year praising God, I asked myself: *How can we continue to be effective?*

I had jotted down notes for that Sunday's message, the next in a series I was giving on "How to Feed Your Faith with Optimism." These notes were on "Five Ways to Preach a Positive Message on a Negative Topic" that I needed to cover that week.

Also on my desk was a packet of materials we give couples preparing to be married in our church. I was to meet with a young couple, Matt and Linda (not their real names), about their wedding ceremony at which I was to officiate. While awaiting their arrival, I found myself thumbing through both the growth statistics and the marriage packet. The phone buzzer rang, indicating that the couple had arrived.

As they entered the room, I immediately recognized them as a young couple who had talked with me after a service several months earlier. They'd been living together for some time. He was about 30, with long, well-groomed brown hair. She was in her mid-30s and looked like Cher, the rock singer. She was wearing very high heels and was dressed in black.

When they took their seats, I glanced over their Taylor-Johnson Temperament Analysis that we share with all couples. Some of the other materials in their premarital packet had already been checked by another pastor on our team. When we got around to the spiritual values portion, I asked if either of them had been raised in church.

Matt answered, "No, not really, Pastor. I went to Sunday School a couple of times when I was young. But because my folks didn't go, I didn't stick long."

Linda then spoke. "My aunt was Catholic. We went to Mass for quite a while, really. Most of us kids went with her. We stopped, though, because my dad was Presbyterian or something. We didn't go much after that."

Glancing over at Matt, Linda asked, "Are you going to tell him?"

Matt replied, "I guess so. We actually met the Lord about 18 years ago at a Jesus People rally. However, we never found a church we could relate to."

I asked. "Well, how long have you been coming here?"

I glanced at Matt to see if he was going to comment. He obviously wasn't, so Linda answered. "Well, we began to get convicted about the way we're living. We don't know a whole lot about the Bible, but our folks are bothered by our living together.

"So we asked around about where we should go to church, because we wanted to get our lives on track spiritually before we got married. One of our friends suggested we come to your congregation. He said we'd be able to handle it here okay and you probably wouldn't run us off."

"Well, how have you liked it so far?" I asked.

I braced myself for the response, thinking it might be negative. Matt's answer was a pleasant surprise.

"I can't believe it! You're the first pastor and this is the first church I've been able to relate to," he replied, grinning from ear to ear.

Linda added, "Yeah, everything seems so spiritual. I remember church being so negative. I can't believe the message you shared on Sunday on 'How to Feed Your Faith with Optimism.' It was so pertinent to the life we're facing!" Her enthusiasm was obvious.

Matt continued. "Yeah, you know, we've got problems we need to get fixed up, but you don't seem anxious to run us down about them."

As we continued our conversation, I wrote down several of their anecdotal stories next to the message on my note pad about "Five Ways to Preach a Positive Message on a Negative Topic." I decided then that I would speak next on "How to Focus on an Optimistic Gospel That Transforms Lives," and penned a note to myself as well: "Be encouraged, Doug. When it looks as though it isn't going to happen, remember Matt and Linda. It does work!"

My earlier concern had been that I would not compromise the gospel. Yet I had already been dinged a few times by people in our city who implied that I had been preaching only what people wanted to hear. But for myself, I was now utterly convinced that I was preaching the truth of the gospel from a positive angle.

Now the transformation that was occurring in Matt and Linda's lives confirmed to me, once again, that this strategy of preaching truth from a positive angle does work in dealing with the thirty something crowd!

I often put it this way: *Don't tell people what they're not going to do. Tell them who they are in Christ, and the gospel becomes very inviting.*

CHURCH 101

I was asked the other evening in a small leadership gathering by one of our elders why I didn't teach more on tithing.

I responded, "I'm reluctant to do that on Sundays, because we have so many unchurched baby boomers just beginning to find their way back to faith."

Handing over the reins of one's life to the lordship of Jesus doesn't come easily. Since such a step is difficult enough for many, I don't think we need to see how many obstacles we can throw in the way of those who seek to come.

His next question was rather curt. "What's that got to do with anything? It's a principle that I've found true all of my life. It's worked for me. Why can't it work for them?"

"When the bulk of people in churches were Christian and quite sturdy in their approach to a principle-oriented life-style, such a reminder was far more amenable," I replied.

He prodded me further. "Well, don't you believe in giving and tithing?"

"Certainly I do, and Deb and I do tithe. But I also understand that, in our environment on Sundays, the Holy Spirit must take people at their own pace."

Thankfully, we finished this discussion in agreement.

I would much rather share anecdotal stories with our congregation about the joy of giving than present the negative aspects of these topics to them. I find that this approach is a requirement for reaching the baby boomers whom I love.

Our church has actually designed a course we've titled "Church 101," wherein we teach on issues, such as tithing and giving, that have been traditionally taught from the pulpit. These issues are taught from a very grace-oriented perspective and with a high regard for individuals to make their own choice along the way. The response in spiritual growth from those who have completed this course is extraordinarily high, because boomers are looking for a positive reason to grow in the Lord.

We've had to embark on a journey to rediscover the gentle process of conversion that is necessary when dealing with a group that is turned off by negative presentations of church life. Now don't get me wrong. I do believe that the gospel is initially negative to every one of us, yet it is primarily a positive message of God's love made incarnate and extended to each one of us. When you come right down to it, this concept of God becoming man to rescue mankind really *is* good news!

The first time the plan of salvation was presented to me, it came through a young man, who said something like: "Jesus Christ died for your sins because He loves you. 'For God so loved the world, that he gave his only begotten Son, that whosoever believeth in him should not perish, but have everlasting life.'" Then he handed me a tract with only this verse of John 3:16 (*KJV*) on it.

What I *thought* I heard, however, was, "You're a dirty, rotten sinner who hates God, and if you don't change, you're going to burn in hell!"

After all, Paul did warn us that the Cross would be a stumbling block—something that doesn't make a lot of sense until you experience Christ. Let's face it: We'd all prefer acts of power that would irrefutably convince us that God is real than to *hear* the message of the Cross.

My point is that the message of the gospel is a wrenching experience for both the totally unchurched and even the nominal Christian. Handing over the reins of your life to the lordship of Jesus doesn't come easily. Since such a step is difficult enough for many, I don't think we need to see how many obstacles we can throw in the way of those who seek to come.

Therefore, one of the best ways to make certain that Christ's message of salvation is heard is to present it with *a positive approach to Christianity*. So when I prepare for Sunday's message, I often write at the top of my notes: *"These people have heard enough bad news this week. What good news does this message have for them today?"*

I've found that nothing beats a balance of good news and truth. In these times, people are well prepared to respond to the gospel of Jesus Christ. According to the Princeton Religion Research Center's 1988 study, titled "The Unchurched American Ten Years Later":

- Between the ages of 25 and 29, 41 percent of the people said they *might* return to church as an active member.
- Between the ages of 30 and 49, 30 percent said that there was a possibility they *might* become a church member.[3]

This study was based on those who had ceased to attend church at the time they were being interviewed. Yet these statistics show a high level of openness to return to church. I'm quite convinced that one of the reasons people are slow in following their heart back to church is that they're looking first for a positive place to which they can return.

MAKING IT EASIER TO TAKE THOSE FIRST STEPS

My personal conviction is that Jesus Christ came to make it easier for people to return to God.

I highly recommend to other churches and congregations an exercise that we use at Eastside Church. We will often work through a self-analysis by asking this question: *Are we making it difficult for unbelievers and nominal Christians to respond to church life by what we do?*

Recently, when our congregation's presbytery gathered, a group of 300 to 400 leaders met in small groups to give input into decision-making that affects long-term issues of our congregation. These groups help me assess how effective we are in leading our church.

One of their comments that filtered back to me was very helpful. They had observed that some of our children's classes weren't marked properly. As a result, many parents attending our church for the first time were experiencing confusion as to where to place their children. This difficulty was making people hesitate to come back a second time.

We also noted in our self-analysis that, for a season in our church life, we gathered in circles on Sunday mornings and prayed. Yet, numbers of unchurched people visiting Eastside and sitting with us in those circles felt quite constrained when they found themselves called upon to pray. We then ceased this practice and, instead, have asked people to prepare their hearts to pray on Wednesday night, thereby making it easier for those who are taking their initial steps toward

Jesus Christ as visitors on Sunday mornings. Our Wednesday night services are called "Believers in Action."

Some areas to examine, in terms of whether we're making it difficult or easier for people are:

- Is the tone of the message positive, uplifting and optimistic?
- Is there anything about our facility that makes it difficult for people to be a part of our church?
- Do the parking facilities make it easier or difficult for people to respond?

We wholeheartedly desire that the tone and quality of our messages and the presentation of our church life make it easy for those who want to find their way back to church.

IN REVIEW

Practical Concerns

The congregations who will reap from the flood of baby boomers returning to church will have the following characteristics in their basic presentation of the gospel message of Jesus Christ:

- The gospel will be presented in predominantly optimistic tones.
- These congregations will create opportunities for church events, programs and support groups that will help people to deal practically with their problems.
- These congregations will have a high regard for the sensitivity of the unchurched and nominal Christians in their midst.

- The majority of Christian discipleship training will take place in small-group settings. Vital issues of church life—such as ·tithing, giving, church structure and discipline—will be dealt with in settings where they can be shared in such a way as not to exceed the rate of growth in an individual's life.
- These congregations will have a great deal of skill developing an environment that allows the Holy Spirit to clean up people and to move them ahead at a pace that He is happy with, invariably a pace which these individuals can handle.
- These congregations will be sinner-friendly. Such an attitude will, in turn, force a networking in churches as never before. Very likely, high levels of drug addiction, sexual addiction and fiscal mismanagement will be evident, circumstances that will put a great deal of pressure on churches.

  These churches will learn quickly that both alcoholics and drug addicts have an 85 percent chance of a relapse during their first year of sobriety. Such individuals can be adequately healed only in an optimistic environment.
- These churches will also require leaders who possess great mental and emotional strength, sturdiness and a high level of character. In addition, this influx of unchurched and nominal Christians will require a strong, highly moral membership. So a lot of training and emphasis will be needed to develop strong principles of leadership.

Practical Suggestions

1. Develop optimistic service formats.
2. Develop support groups to allow for the care of people with serious problems.

3. Develop programs that will make visitors in any state or condition feel welcome and at home.

4. Train ushers and children's workers in the art of graciousness and the expression of a grace-oriented, tolerant, loving and accepting approach to Christianity.

5. Establish a regular pattern of self-evaluation. Ask such questions as:

   • Is the message we present being received and understood as being optimistic?

   • Are people receiving encouragement from our congregational life so that they can confidently face some of the harder issues of life?

   • Are we expressing compassion and solution-oriented Christianity in the face of some of our community's greatest tragedies, such as rampant abortion, drug addiction and marital breakups?

   In this regular practice of self-analysis it is most important to make certain that we continue to stay on a positive track.

6. Pastors ought to evaluate their messages regularly by asking themselves if they have developed a satisfactory ratio between the positive and negative issues of Scripture.

My personal feeling is that baby boomers will need an environment with *at least three positive statements to every negative one in order to thrive.* An appropriate verse for missions and the presentation of church life in our time, therefore, is *"a cheerful look brings joy to the heart and good news gives health to the bones"* (Prov. 15:30).

POSITIVE ABOUT GIVING

The decade of the 1990s can provide the greatest open window yet for the Church to seize the focus of an entire generation. Churches can use this great opportunity to lead a generation which is still very altruistic and believes strongly in their own destiny and mission.

Yet a great void of leadership exists in this generation. So boomers are looking for leaders who will help them to understand better the relationship between the spiritual and the material. The Church can provide this much-needed leadership, but will it? For it to do so, the Church must first be willing to challenge and strike a chord for God in the sense of destiny that fills this group of baby boomers.

Let's talk further about this important matter of leadership and giving in the next chapter.

Notes
1. Landon Jones, *Great Expectations: America and the Baby Boom Generation* (New York: Ballantine Books, 1986).
2. *Emerging Trends*, vol. 2, no. 3 (Princeton: Princeton Religion Research Center, March 1989).
3. "The Unchurched American Ten Years Later" (Princeton: Princeton Religion Research Center, 1988).

12

IS OUR MONEY ALL THEY WANT?

*"I'd like to live life like a poor man
with lots of money."*
—Pablo Picasso[1]

SOMETIMES the pace of life and the impact of our culture gives me the feeling of being dragged down the road against my will to face ever-new realities. This experience, says author Alvin Toffler in his best-seller, is called "future shock." But whatever it is called, it occasionally makes me feel—as a church leader—a little bit the way a dog named "Tattoo" must have felt on a certain occasion:

> Tattoo, the basset hound, never intended to go for an evening run, but had no choice when his owner shut his leash in the car door and took off for a drive—with Tattoo still outside the vehicle!
>
> Tacoma [Washington] Police motorcycle officer, Terry Filbert, was driving near North 21st and Adam Street about 7:25 P.M., Wednesday, when he noticed a vehicle that appeared to have something dragging from it. As Filbert passed the vehicle, he noticed that the dragging item was a basset hound on a leash, "picking them up and putting them down as fast as he could."
>
> Filbert gave chase as the car turned eastbound on North 21st and finally stopped, but not before the poor dog reached the speed of 20-25 m.p.h. "and rolled several times."
>
> The car's occupants, a man and a woman, jumped out when Filbert told them they were dragging a dog. The couple became distressed and began calling, "Tattoo! Tattoo!"
>
> Tattoo, eight months old, appeared uninjured, but Filbert suggested the couple take him to the

animal clinic to be checked out. No citation was issued.[2]

Yes, the times move fast, bringing changes for everyone. But for us baby boomers, the processes of change seem accelerated at every stage of our lives. Yesterday's realities quickly become today's obsolescences. This is especially true in the realm of finances, as more expected and unexpected turns in our culture loom on the horizon.

MONEY—A LARGE I$$UE FOR BOOMERS

We boomers are facing several new realities about our money. First, our expectations are becoming tempered, as our actual earned income is less than that of our parents at every stage of life.[3]

Our income, however, is expected to increase collectively in the 1990s. By the year 2000, we boomers will, in fact, account for 40 percent of the nation's spending power. Household income of boomers now in the 35 to 40 age-group is predicted to reach 90 percent of all U.S. income by the turn of this century.[4]

But the steadily rising cost of living has chewed up most of the income advances in the past. And who knows what the immediate future—the next decade—holds for boomers?

All the dialogue about our economy's uncertainty and the strident teaching by Christian financial advisors to get out of debt have impacted this generation greatly. But given the financial constraints on our generation, only a comparative few have been able to do much economically without credit. Many of us have just finished paying off our first washing machine.

Within our own congregation, I've noted the younger boomers have been especially pressed by the inflation of the 1970s and the 1980s. The dilemma of being in a short money-supply situation, where our middle-class American life-style generally can be afforded by only a two-income family—that, combined with the reality that once child care is paid for, the second income is greatly diminished—are causing a great deal of concern and frustration about money.

So money is a very large issue for the thirty something crowd, second only to the matter of health, according to a generational survey of Peter Hart Associates for *Rolling Stone* magazine in 1987: "After health, boomers consider their money their chief concern, and retirement money at that. The majority of the generation that is still in its 30s and is often stereotyped as 'Yuppie Spenders,' is now focusing on retirement."[5]

The financial dilemma of boomers and the pressure we experience from it is somewhat self-inflicted. For, in many ways, we're trying to live a life-style that's unattainable for us. And trying to attain the unattainable is a frustrating experience for us all.

If church leaders are insensitive to this financial dilemma dogging baby boomers, great injustices will be done, and our churches will not only become unappealing, but especially damaging to younger boomers.

Boomers—A Challenge to Church Fund-Raising

I'll never forget when I stood before our congregation on Tuesday evening following the great stock market crash of Black Monday on October 20, 1987. We were just making some progress on our new building program, and we had slated this Tuesday evening as our second fund-raising dinner. I really don't like fund-raising dinners anyway, but reality causes those of us with dreams to face the real world at times, for it was vitally necessary to raise approximately $100,000 just to get this project off the ground.

Church methods of fund-raising do not speak to our felt needs. So church leaders need to reexamine their methodology in this area. We boomers tend to be very consumer-minded. Before we give to an organization, we usually ask, "What's in it for me?"

Unfortunately, the evening news had been filled with traumatic reports of this crash. It would have been no surprise to me if only a few people had attended the event. Instead, to my very pleasant surprise, the dinner was well attended, though principally by people from our congregation in the 50-plus age bracket. Praise God that they were part of our congregation at that time. They were a great encouragement to me!

I learned a great deal about the peace of God that evening as I stood up to share our financial need. The angry reports from the press made it difficult for people to respond financially to this need, because they were gripped by the fear that their life-style could possibly erode from under them, a fear which caused many people to tighten up their money belts. Within a few months, however, a rational perspective returned and we moved on.

Financial frustration may be one of the reasons why the preponderance of church organizations still cater to the 50-plus age-group. Most pastors I've talked to admit quickly that it's the older age-group in their congregations that carries a far higher percentage per capita of the financial load. We've found this to be true in our own congregation as well. Reaching boomers at this point is not yet cost-effective—in the generally accepted use of the term.

Why?

Nonparticipation Factors
Three factors, I believe, are part of the reason for the lower financial participation of baby boomers in local churches and Christian organizations:

1. Apart from the financial pressure from trying to meet expectations that can't be met, boomers are finding it untenable that we are behind our parents economically at each stage of life.

2. Boomers have an undeveloped understanding of the relationship between the spiritual and the material. Conversely, I have not found this to be so with our folks' generation—the generation that led us in church life. The concept of giving, on the basis of responsibility and biblical requisites, is clearly understood by my parent's generation.

But because of my generation's extreme consumer mentality, it isn't something that we grasp at all. It is difficult to explain to boomers the need for giving. Our perceived nonparticipation financially is perhaps due to the fact that we've grown up in the era of great government subsidies and student loans. Consequently, we have been lulled into thinking that, somehow, everything will be magically taken care of.

3. Church methods of fund-raising do not speak to our felt needs. So church leaders need to reexamine their methodology in this area. We boomers tend to be very consumer-minded. Before we give to an organization, we usually ask: "What's in it for me?"

Crisis Fund-raising

Also, I've noted that one of the styles used by churches and Christian organizations for many years is what I would call "crisis fund-raising." This crisis motivation method, while quite effective in the churches of our parents for the last several decades, will *not* appeal at all to the people of my generation. The Black Monday crisis of the stock market in 1987 has strongly confirmed this to me.

I am convinced that people my age don't really believe they can give of their resources, and are a little shell-shocked by all the dire predictions of doom and gloom in our American economy. So any church's future approach to finances must be devoid of crisis situations and dire predictions that God will remove His blessing if we don't give, because boomers are *not* motivated by these tactics.

The Scandal Factor

Still another reason that makes raising funds from boomers difficult are the financial scandals of the late 1980s, particularly the PTL scandal involving Jim and Tammy Faye Bakker. Even the illegal inside stock-trading situation of Ivan F. Boesky has jaded our opinion of people who ask us for money.

I watched, with great interest, the Larry King show one evening in 1989, when Pat Robertson, founder of CBN (the Christian Broadcasting Network) and former host of the "700 Club," was being interviewed about the "guilty" verdict, following Jim Bakker's conviction. Larry King asked Pat if he expected much more intervention in the affairs of other Christian organizations, such as CBN.

Pat's response was, "Yes, I do, but I'm opposed to any more state intervention in the affairs of Christian organizations."

I think it was apparent to most observers that the move toward more government intervention has definitely abated. Instead, greater issues concerning Lithuania and Russia, the razing of the Berlin Wall after 29 years and environmental issues have taken center stage. As a Christian leader, I too am really quite relieved that church scandals have moved away from the front page.

When we commenced negotiations to refinance our new facility, our banker looked at me intently and asked if the scandals of the 1980s had impacted our ability to raise money as we had done in the past.

That was a great question, which I hadn't really thought about up to that point. As best we could tell, the scandals had not directly impacted our weekly giving, but our local radio program had been impacted significantly. In fact, for that reason, we decided to back off somewhat in developing our radio outreach ministry.

In addition, we have found ourselves making more careful effort in presenting our financial planning. We have also been examining our own hearts. Are we handling our resources with the utmost of integrity?

I'm happy to report that, to the best of our knowledge, we are. We've taken a number of steps to ensure that our accountability remains intact.

Meeting our banker's intent gaze, I replied that we had noted one thing: Our margin of error had been greatly reduced.

The monetary scandals of the 1980s, combined with the pressure of meeting expectations, have greatly reduced the margin of error that leaders can have when presenting money issues, especially to boomers. That margin of error continues to shrink and is now very thin.

Just how thin is it? I don't have any existing scientific information, but my own perception is that most boomers in our church will basically tolerate—at the most—two hard-hitting fund-raising presentations that are imbalanced. In the area of finances, their tolerance for what would be perceived to be inefficacious manipulation is *that* thin.

I truly believe that, without a great deal of planning and long-term foresight, boomers could be turned off by evangelical churches, unless we learn to think through carefully the process of how to raise funds.

MISSIONS, BEWARE!

Scene: Conference Room, Eastside Foursquare Church
Date: Mid-1980s

Six of us sat around the conference table. Notepads were stacked on our left and monthly financial reports had been placed directly before each of us. To our right sat a stack of plans to expand our new sanctuary, along with our missions strategy for the coming year.

"Why don't these people give to missions offerings when we have them?" complained John, whose face was turning red. His frustration was apparent in both his appearance and in his tone of voice.

Gordon spoke up. "They don't want to."

Les, whose job it was to promote special offerings for missions, quickly offered, "I've got some new ideas to get the word [about missions] to them. By the way, 'them' is us."

"The last church I belonged to, our missions budget nearly equaled our salaries," added Bill on my right.

I didn't want to look at him. Discussing another church's performance really burned me up. But now wasn't the time to react to or engage in a tirade about comparisons; not now when we had obtained only half of our missions budget and had to finance our missions commitment out of our regular cash flow. After all, we were sincere men and women, desiring to figure out why we had to dip into our operating budget again to fulfill our missions commitment.

John started again. "Man, we've had missionaries and missions directors speaking to the congregation. This is pitiful. There's something really wrong with our MO [method of operation]."

Turning to Dave, I asked, "What do you think the issue is?"

Dave responded, "I agree with Gordon. We don't want to give to faceless missionaries."

Bill blurted out, "I've been in church for 25 years and I've never been in one that didn't have a missions heart. What are we going to do, Pastor?"

"Dave, how old were you when the Vietnam War was raging?" I asked.

"All of 21—and fighting like mad to miss it too," replied Dave.

Gordon jumped in: "I was 21 too, but I was around when the VC [Viet Cong] were just outside our surveillance camps."

The others sat silently. I realized that both John and Bill had matured around the end of World War II.

"What's that got to do with anything?" Dave asked me. He hoped I was up to something, that I had an idea.

"Well," I answered, "I've got a hunch that most of our congregation, myself included, lived through the Vietnam era and watched our older cousins go and do the fighting and saw America embarrassed every night on the evening news while we did our homework."

Dave chimed in. "Yeah, I remember the TV coverage—the body counts, the comments and promises of Presidents Kennedy, Johnson and Nixon."

Larry added: "Yeah, it really did impact me!"

I continued. "Well, I don't think we can buy into the idea anymore that it is America's duty to save the world."

This conversation continued for quite some time. Eventually, we all reached a consensus, though I'm not sure that Bill or John were completely satisfied. But at least they understood.

We all concluded that we were dealing with a group of people who had seen, via TV, every part of the globe since their childhood. So, missions weren't anything too distant for them.

We boomers also feel guilty about being the "ugly American." And the Japanese seem to be outperforming us in a variety of areas, so we just don't feel all that confident about ourselves anymore.

I think the comment of the night came from Gordon, when he said, "Yeah, you show me a white American missionary telling colored people what to do and I'm turned off."

"Exactly!" David agreed.

John, by that time, had become interested. "Are you serious?"

"Yes, we really are, John. So what do we do?"

John's reply was thoughtful. "Well, I think we'll have to be very creative. We'll have to measure our obstacles with our group, and we'll have to determine that missions are the godly thing to do, that it's God's will for us to be a missions church.

"It's the call of God on our congregation, but we'll have to face those obstacles, which are many. It will possibly take years to build a missions mentality into this group."

FROM CYNICISM TO GIVING

I used to believe that the money issue wasn't a big factor in church life. But now that I pastor a fairly large church with a decent mortgage, my perspective has changed. The reality of leading and desiring to nurture people have forced me to face the fact that *good care costs money*. It is my task as a leader to share this assumption with our congregation.

As a leader, I've also had to face the fact that *the New Testament reminds us several times that giving and tithing are part of true spiritual maturity*. I don't wish to be the kind of leader who would cater so much to the baby boomers' cultural hesitancy to fund or to make life so easy for them that they wouldn't mature in the area of using their money and resources for the furtherance of God's Kingdom on Earth. Jesus made it quite clear that if we can't handle mammon—the treasures of this world—how can we ever handle the true treasures of the Kingdom of God?

So what can we do?

Being a baby boomer myself, as well as leading a group of wonderfully generous people, I think there are other issues that could help boomers to get beyond their basic cynicism. And I say that, even though in our church, by an unscientific method, we have found the issue of offerings to be one of the greater obstacles for boomers in our area returning to church.

So how can churches deal with the issue of boomers and money? Having been thrust into the leadership of a rapidly growing church, I have a little feel for raising funds, though I have had to learn it the hard way.

Finances always follow true, caring ministries...If we boomers have had our needs met through one of your programs and have benefited from your pastoral caring and concern, we are more likely to respond financially.

During the first several years of our church's existence, I really didn't want people to feel pressed to give money. Still, I was realistic enough to know, as all leaders ultimately do, that it costs money to expand and nurture a church.

At one point we simply placed a box at the back of the gymnasium where we were meeting. We announced that we wouldn't raise offerings in our services anymore; that if people wanted to present their tithes and offerings to the church, they could place them in that box and we would praise the Lord for whatever we were given.

This experiment fell on its face in about two months because we were going broke. I think this experiment failed for these reasons:

- We had not adequately taught the concept of giving.
- I eventually found myself, because of the pressure of needs, reminding our congregation about the box at the back of the gym and doing brief teachings about giving, something I had already been doing when we had previously passed bags for collecting the offering.

Several of our leaders suggested that we return to passing bags, because we were still having to do so much explaining about the box anyway. Though it's possible this experiment would have worked then, it certainly wouldn't today, now that we have thousands of people attending our services. There would be quite a line at that box, to be sure. And I've since decided that passing bags is fine; right now, it expedites the matter of finances quite effectively.

I share this example only to describe the search I've gone through to deal with the entire issue of financing and raising funds for our church. As a pastor, it is still my task to deal with the issues that relate to finances when facing boomers. So my immediate concerns in this area are:

- How can I help boomers to reach over the hurdle of the pressure of our unmet expectations? There isn't enough money to live up to the life-style we're accustomed to. So how are we to respond to giving?
- As a church leader, I constantly try to bring about a biblical and reasonable understanding concerning the relationship between the spiritual and the material.
- For several years, I have tried different approaches regarding giving and tithing to help boomers to understand the joy and value of giving to their local

congregation. My methods have necessarily been adjusted a number of times in order to inspire boomer participation in the financial side of our church life.

How Can We Talk About the "M" Word?

Faced with the constant need for facility expansion and a strong desire to plant other churches, as well as having to deal honestly with the costs of better care, I've had to ask these questions over and over:

- How can I respond to the people of my generation in such a way that they will want to participate in giving in a way that's healthy for them?
- How can I talk about resources in such a way that it won't turn off the unchurched who visit our congregation?

While we were in the midst of our fund-raising, I made a deliberate effort to visit several churches around the country to ask pastors and staff people how they raise funds and what other ideas they might have about fund-raising that allows them to stay true to their values. Given the climate of the 1980s and the 1990s, how do they still raise operating funds?

I give credit here to the basic statements and ideas I gleaned from conducting this very unscientific survey. I've found that these ideas work well in appealing to boomers to respond and grow in the area of giving and tithing:

Put Faces on Needs. Boomers respond very reluctantly to institutions; they're not likely to give money for bricks. When we began raising funds for our new facility, we talked about "our children's building." In all our literature, video and in-person presentations, we emphasized the *people* who would be using this facility, rather than the facility itself. Buildings are not perceived to be a long-term investment by boomers; people are.

Concentrate on Meeting People's Needs. Finances always follow true, caring ministries. People understand the need to respond financially when their lives have been truly transformed. Getting the cart before the horse can be a very painful realization, especially with thirty something people. If we boomers have had our needs met through one of your programs and have benefited from your pastoral caring and concern, we are more likely to respond financially.

A system of teaching must be inaugurated about giving and tithing that will allow boomers to have their needs met in your setting *prior* to their being thrust into the growing dimension of learning to give sacrificially.

Teach Giving in Smaller Settings and Classes. A number of times our church has had to deal with the issue of trimming and/or adjusting a program, in terms of timing, due to a lack of finances.

At these times, someone invariably asks how well the church is giving. My response is always that our people are giving generously. In fact, our church growth expert, Dr. Lucky Klopp, has advised me that, per capita, our congregation gives above the average.

Someone else will usually ask what percentage of our people do the bulk of the giving. As is usual with most churches, 17 percent to 20 percent of our people carry the financial load of this congregation. At that point, pressure tactics are generally exerted on me to give a sermon series on giving and tithing.

However, I've never been able to follow this suggestion. Many of the unchurched baby boomers who have been drawn to our congregation are living under the pressure of unmet expectations and jaded perspectives as a result of the church scandals in the late 1980s, and they are *certain* that all we want is their money.

I've found that a more preferable path for us to take is to talk about giving and tithing in smaller settings. Let me illustrate some of those settings. In our membership class, which is titled "Church 101," we outline the basic fundamentals and philosophy of our church life. One of the sections in the class—usually taught to no more than 30 to 40 people at a time—is on tithing, missions giving and sacrificial giving.

We've found that this system has been quite effective. Because these folks are already comfortable in our church, they respond quite readily to its needs. Though this idea may not be all that new, its style of presentation is fun and very carefully shared.

When it addresses the area of fund-raising for our new building, we've developed a group of people we call "presbyters." They are leaders in our church who meet with groups of 10 to 15 people. When we recently considered expanding our facility to include a wedding chapel and a youth center, instead of talking about them publicly, I first have our presbyters meet with hundreds of people in our congregation to share with them the cost of these additions.

Prepare Cassettes. Using cassette tapes to present financial needs is very valuable. Through a tape I can say to my boomer friends, "Look, I don't want to take service time to talk to you about money because you've come to church to receive from God. You probably realize that it takes money to operate this church, so I've prepared a cassette tape for you to listen to at home, which will help you to become aware of some of our needs around here. Please listen to it and pray about it. I think you'll be blessed by knowing a little more about how we operate."

Baby boomers perceive a message on a cassette as a great idea. The tape allows me to avoid the misinterpretation of being viewed as a fund-raiser and yet I'm able to get across the message of our needs.

Publish a Yearly Budget. Here are the three methods that we've found to be very effective in helping us to grow in the area of finances. They do take a little longer, but I believe they have more of a long-term impact:

- We publish our budget figures at least twice yearly on our video screen.
- We use a pie graph to show where the funds given us have been directed and spent.
- We also publish these figures in our Sunday bulletins and note the amount given that year to the current date.

We find that it is very helpful to put the information out there for all to see. People do want to know where the needs are. And these are great ways to make people aware of what's happening without our harping on the subject.

Model a Giving Life-style. I truly believe that if church leaders are committed to being strong givers, that their attitude, without cajoling or reminding, will be assimilated throughout the entire church.

Consider Delayed Development. It's a fact that, with boomers in growing churches, multiple services will be necessary. This is a new concept in the church world.

Sometimes parking limitations have necessitated multiple services. Another factor for holding multiple services has been to avoid debt acquisition. From my own experience in boomer churches, they are still necessary, even when a large debt is assumed.

Delayed development is a necessary perspective in various churches. I believe that church building development in the 1990s will take quite a bit longer than it has in past decades. Longer lead times to work through the building permit process will be a factor, but still another factor is that it will simply take longer to get your idea across to obtain the necessary financial support for development.

Develop Hands-on Missions Giving. In missions giving, allow opportunities for hands-on participation. Boomers want to "own" what they give to, which is frustrating for missions leaders. As a pastor, I understand why field workers are already in the field. Organizational commitments and budgets have already been acquired. Computer systems have been purchased and then, at this point, boomers say, "But we don't want to give to your institution."

We've found that using videos in our services has helped immensely to bring missionaries working out in the field right into our services. We ask missions organizations with whom we're affiliated to send us videos of their field work so that our congregation will desire to get involved. These videos are shown Sunday mornings and Wednesday nights.

It's truly exciting to see a missionary in Nepal, for instance, who has suffered for his faith, share his vision for touching the kids in his care in real, meaningful ways. Seeing a video like this really touches the hearts of its viewers. Then, because boomers love to give to people with faces, they will want to get involved.

Missions organizations would do well to develop a financial base that would permit lay missionary teams to share in ministries around the world. This has been an excellent method for imparting hands-on experience to people. I believe it will become a necessary operating procedure for any missions organization interested in using boomer dollars in their outreach.

As mentioned earlier, the white guy in the pith helmet who runs around the jungles of Africa telling blacks what to do is no longer an inviting sight. Nor do boomers perceive that it is up to America to save the world. However, boomers do get enthusiastic about missions that will allow them hands-on contact and experience.

Practice Clustering for Burdens and Passions. Graham Kerr, formerly known as the "Galloping Gourmet," is a valued member of our congregation. He has devised a concept he calls "clustering." It consists of a group of 5 to 15 people with like burdens and visions for a particular need in their church, in their community or on the international scene.

We are presently developing such a program to implement this concept fully in our church. It works like this: If someone has a burden for, say, an Indian tribe in Northern Canada, a board depicting that tribe is displayed in our church foyer. Those interested in that area of ministry to which they feel drawn by the Lord then place stickers on the board with their names and phone numbers.

These stickers are collected by a staff person who networks with these individuals and develops them into a cluster group, which would then respond to that tribe's needs by giving of their time, prayers and finances. This arrangement creates hands-on ownership of that particular ministry. People tend to give to what they feel they own, and are more likely to give on a long-term basis to that in which they have participated.

We've seen this sort of thing happen a number of times to people in our congregation who have gone on extensive missionary trips. We plan to increase this number by 30 percent a year over the next five years, as we are desirous that our people be resources in all areas of their lives. Boomers will be able to participate in these missionary ventures with hands-on involvement.

Make Giving Fun. "Fun" and "experience" are two vital words to boomers. Let's allow them the joy and the fun of experiencing giving.

When raising funds for our new building, we showed a series of video tapes on the project that were really funny. I genuinely felt that humor was necessary to help people understand the joy that can be realized by giving. After all, as Paul said in 2 Cor. 9:7, God loves the person who gives hilariously.

One of my favorite presentations was based on an Isuzu truck ad. You may have seen it yourself. If not, perhaps you can picture it as I describe our version of this ad.

We used the ad of Joe Isuzu trying to sell a truck while making outrageous claims. As he makes his pitch, subtitles flash under his picture, saying, "He's lying." For example, in one ad, the Isuzu manufacturers had Joe say, "You get a free truck if you immediately run down to your Isuzu dealer."

But underneath, the caption read, "He's lying. The truck costs $15,000."

In our takeoff on this video ad, one of our assistant pastors dressed up like Joe Isuzu, drove up in front of our partially completed facility in an Isuzu van, jumped out and unrolled our plans for the completed facility. A picture of the cathedral Notre Dame de Paris appeared on the screen.

Our Joe Isuzu impersonator said, "This is what our completed facility will look like."

But the subtitle underneath read, "He's lying. It will actually look like this." The architect's rendition of our completed facility then appeared on the screen. Then the Joe Isuzu impersonator appeared again and said, "The exciting part about our new building is that it's already paid for."

The subtitle underneath now read, "He's lying. We need $250,000 by July."

People got the point. It was humorous and exciting, and we had fun doing it. I think the key factor here was that it was fun.

Giving ought to be fun as well as meaningful. Funds shouldn't be raised at a pace that is faster than is possible for givers to have fun while doing it. I want to do even more Joe Isuzu ads like those we've already done, but I haven't as yet been able to convince our Isuzu impersonator to do them.

Make Accountability Systems Known. In these times it is important that people know how your church finances are handled. In our church I explain regularly that our books are balanced by an outside accounting firm and that, each month, we turn in financial statements to our denominational headquarters.

In addition, our finances are scrutinized by our church council of seven people, who were elected to the council by our congregation. According to our affiliation and bylaws, I do not sign any checks myself, and we operate on a budget. People appreciate this kind of accountability, especially people with the gift of giving no matter what their age-group.

Remember That Vision Precedes Resources. This is an important lesson. Motivating people to give involves the ability to share a vision. Boomers especially want to fulfill a great destiny.

Challenge them with the vision of your church and you won't have to beg them for money. I believe the Scripture clearly teaches that a vision always precedes the release of resources.

Cultivate Baby Boomer Hearts and Time. Do this sincerely and then you'll have their money. Patience is important when it comes to parting boomers from their money.

Get their hearts committed to where your church is heading. Show them your love. Challenge them to invest their time and life into what you're doing. Love their kids—and their money will follow.

People have various interests. Only a few boomers will be interested initially in helping to pay for your building's heat and lights. But they will understand those needs better and help you with them, if you first help them with whatever needs to be done for them.

It is important to create and offer multiple types of opportunities for giving; such as special offerings for benevolence, for missions, for special group outreaches, for evangelism and for a building fund. Different ideas and opportunities turn different people on, so by presenting boomers with multiple choices for giving, you are more likely to obtain their participation.

Show Gratitude. Thank your congregation for what they do give at least twice as often as you ask them to give. I know I certainly appreciate a thank-you and a note of appreciation. So I make it a regular habit to thank our congregation for their generous giving.

Each quarter we mail out acknowledgments of the amount each person has given, along with a thank you note or card from me. I really do value each person's contribution and I think each one deserves thanks. I know that when I receive my own thank-you note, I feel motivated to give more.

Tell People What's in It for Them. Boomers are very interested in being happy, so make them happy by telling them what's in it for them.

When I say, "People usually give when they know what's in it for them," this grates against some of my pastor friends. Whether we like it or not, our American psyche is built around this kind of self-centeredness. I don't think Paul or Malachi backed away from making it clear that there's a blessing in store for those who do give to God and His work on earth.

I enjoy telling anecdotes about how good I felt when I gave to this or that endeavor, as well as sharing stories from others about how well things went for them after giving to a cause. In fact, I make it a habit to collect positive stories about giving when money is involved in church life.

Already, there are too many negative examples out there. So I honestly believe that positive examples will always help defray the damage done by scandals.

Before discussing the matter of giving with your congregation, it will bring more dividends if church leaders take the time to describe what will be gained by participating in a particular offering. Just a few possibilities of this type are the feeling of participation, the ability to continue to enjoy what we already have, the spiritual release that comes with the function of every spiritual gift—of which giving is one, the joy of seeing our kids in a clean, attractive facility or the reassuring knowledge that starving people overseas are being fed.

Yes, it really does help people to know that it is to their own advantage to participate in giving.

Address Unmet Financial Expectations. For boomers, church leaders need to address the area of unmet expectations in the financial area. Our church, for instance, regularly offers financial seminars for those who wish to attend.

From time to time, my messages deal with the concept of *dematerializing* our lives, such as finding release from the frustration of wanting two cars when only one can be afforded or from desiring a three-car garage when a one-car garage is all that the budget will allow.

Teaching baby boomers how to have a realistic life-style and how to manage their resources from the standpoint of a Christian value system is not only very helpful to them, but actually necessary for those who are facing the frustration of stunted, stagnated life-styles and the lack of any discernable progress toward goals, whether realistic or fanciful.

Share the Spiritual Nature of Giving. When it comes to giving, I tell a couple of times a month how the material use of our resources affects our spiritual growth. I do this through brief, succinct statements.

Remember, boomers were schooled during the 1960s to believe that the spiritual is found only in the ethereal. They have also been strongly encouraged by their worldview to regard most material things as evil. These, by the way, are the same things which Mom and Dad worked hard to acquire.

Mentally, baby boomers reacted to and rejected material possessions, though they are actually quite materially oriented. Yet, when it comes to being spiritual, boomers somehow don't figure that spirituality involves responding with their resources in the material realm. Boomers need you to teach them about the spiritual nature of participating in the material world.

MOVING FROM GIVING TO SERVICE AND LEADERSHIP

Hopefully, some of these ideas will help boomers to be more responsive, an ever-fluid issue. Different seasons of our church life have required different responses. Unique attitudes exist toward giving when it comes to the boomer generation versus other generations. To overlook this quality could cripple them a great deal spiritually and possibly cause them to miss out on the many glorious opportunities awaiting their ministry to all the other wonderful people around them.

Notice the progression here. First, Bob and Betty Boomernosky, in their search for a boomer-friendly church were curious, but cautious visitors. They liked what they experienced, so they progressed from being mere visitors to active participants in the full life of the church, as their gifts and talents enabled them to do so. Growing in the faith, they have gone on to become active in ministry, outreach and giving.

Now mature and seasoned Christians, the Boomernoskys are ready for leadership roles in their church. The consumer generation that preceded them in the church is now greying and gradually moving off the scene, handing over leadership to the following generation—their generation, the boomers.

As the torch is passed to younger hands, what are the leadership opportunities that invite and challenge the thirty something generation? How can this vital leadership transition best be accomplished? We'll discuss this important issue in the next and final chapter of this book.

Notes
1. Laurence J. Peter, *Peter's Quotations: Ideas for Our Time* (New York: Bantam Books, 1977), p. 346.
2. Associated Press dispatch, *Tacoma News Tribune,* March 29, 1990.
3. *Boomer Report,* 1, no. 12 (March 1990), 4.
4. *Boomer Report,* 1, no. 1 (April 1989), 6.
5. Peter Hart Associates, generational survey, *Rolling Stone,* 1987.

13
THIRTY SOMETHING AND OUR FUTURE

"The assertion that this generation is somehow special has defined the baby boom from the beginning. It is not the first generation to make this claim, but none has ever said it more forcefully or convincingly."

—Landon Jones[1]

THE baby boom generation is beginning to move into years of power and political impact. Cheryl Russell of American Demographics pronounced a strong prediction, when she said, "Some of you may think you've heard too much about the baby boomer, but you haven't heard anything yet because the generation has just gained the economic and political power to shape events."[2]

BOOMERS—A POTENTIAL POWER FOR MORAL GOOD

Economically, boomers have always been the prized jewel of marketers. And given our sheer numbers, doesn't it seem surprising that we haven't already seized the political scene? Yet, interestingly enough, we boomers have made little effort to harness any of our demographic strength.

But our sheer numbers and demographic strength are not lost on the political power structure. Consequently, boomers are just beginning to become the focus of both parties.

Paula Rinehart, in her article, "The Pivotal Generation," tells the story of Senator Joe Biden's 1984 campaign speech before a group of boomer voters in New Jersey. In this article, she quotes Patrick Caddell, president of Cambridge Survey Research and a consultant to the Democratic Party, as he comments on the boomer reaction to Biden's remarks:

> "Like many of you," Biden said, "I'm 40 years old—and I was drawn to politics by a black man who had a dream at a mall on a steamy August night in Washington."

Biden continued to reflect on the generation's earlier ideals and closed by challenging the group to a reawakening of moral courage and values that went beyond personal gain.

Cadell then observed: "I've been in politics for a long time, but I never saw a reaction like that. These New Jersey voters stood up and applauded—and then they started crying."

He added, "That while boomer value systems may be complicated, their original instincts are still very much intact."[3]

The Democrats don't have a corner on the rush to appeal to boomers. Lee Atwater, Republican Party chairman, said:

The baby boomers have a social conscience. They believe in the equality of women. They're open to change. They're uncomfortable with the gulf that exists between their values and their life-styles. Candidates who understand and try to make values and life-styles work together for this group are going to do very well.[4]

Earth Day in the spring of 1990 was an amazing event to observe. As a nation, we witnessed the issue of environmental protection—which had been on the periphery of our culture for a long time—become a mainstream issue. This change is due in part to the impact of boomers, who have always been very socially conscious, as Lee Atwater has noted.

Patrick Caddell also comments on the social consciousness and desire to change the world that typifies boomers:

This is the generation with the collective sense that they can do great things, yet they are leading a life right now that is fairly mundane in terms of changing the world. Neither political party has been able to reach this generation in a way that will allow it—and its aspiration to change the world—to become a central power force. The one that does will likely be the majority party for the rest of this century.[5]

Now that boomers have aged and have gained more power, we're directing attention to social issues that have been our concerns for a long time. But why aren't we acting on our concerns and making those changes we profess to desire? Why aren't we leading out in the manner that our numbers will permit? Why are we instead leading lives that are "fairly mundane in terms of changing the world?"

LEADERSHIP—A CHALLENGE TO THE CHURCH

It is apparent that the missing ingredient that would unleash this power is leadership. Certainly a leadership void exists in the boomer generation. Nevertheless, baby boomers are looking for leadership.

Will the Church be able to supply that needed leadership? Are we, as a Church, able to fill that leadership void? I sincerely hope so. For, if not, we will hand the reins over to somebody else.

But first, we have to ask ourselves, are our churches ready and able to address some of the issues and concerns that are part of the boomer value system? Will our churches offer vision and values challenging enough to appeal to that latent desire of baby boomers to change the world?

I think the great number of boomers returning to church are subconsciously hoping to find a challenge and something worth committing to, so we can fulfill a desire to have a positive impact on lives. Translated that means *exercising leadership*.

Churches that offer leadership instilled with values and morals, along with a servant's attitude, will have the best chance of capturing the thirty something crowd's attention. Are we in the Church prepared to provide—and share—such leadership?

Could it be that the return of thirty something people to the Church is with the hope that our destiny will be realized through leadership found there? I believe so. And I truly hope all boomers find it.

ACCEPTING THE CHALLENGE

Sharon (not her real name), who belongs to our congregation, is a nurse. She walked up to one of our team pastors after a service and excitedly announced, "I think the Lord is going to let me do what I've dreamed of doing all these years. Do you have anything I can do?"

Our pastor responded, "Well, that depends. What do you see the Lord doing with your life? We do have several job descriptions already prepared. Why don't you share some more details with me."

Sharon was ready for his question and answered, "Pastor, I would really like to make a difference in this church and in the world. We've saved our money for several years now so that we could give an entire year of work to the church. We think that's the right thing to do as Christians.

"We want to make a difference. What do you have for us that would be worth that kind of investment?"

Our team pastor almost leaped. "Boy, have we got a list! Take your pick."

We briefly discussed this encounter at our pastoral team meeting the following week. We had all talked to a number of people who desired taking the same step as Sharon and her husband. As a pastor, I was greatly encouraged that a number of folks my age wanted to prepare for a ministry in which their lives would make a difference.

Are our churches ready and able to address some of the issues and concerns that are part of the boomer value system? Will our churches offer vision and values challenging enough to appeal to that latent desire of baby boomers to change the world?

I'm very optimistic about churches that are willing to be visionary and challenging enough to tap into this boomer energy. We can be part of a blockbuster grass roots movement for the next couple of decades that could be the church's most effective era of ministry yet!

An extremely important key for tapping this energy is *trustworthy and challenging leadership.* The kind of life sacrifice we are talking about here is such a precious commodity that church leaders dare not take advantage of such dedicated people to further their own goals and dreams.

Truly God-serving leadership would rather seek to equip and facilitate people into realizing the dreams which the Lord has placed in their hearts. Of course, this will, at times, mean imparting loving, God-given direction that will best serve the individuals and also be most effective for the strategy and plans of their church.

Through the missions organization with whom we work, we were granted an opportunity in the spring of 1990 to send a medical team, a construction team and a Bible-teaching team to Papua, New Guinea. These teams were to provide medical services and to build churches and dormitories. The expenses of this trip were in excess of $2,000 per person.

Tom (not his real name) is a contractor in our church. He is not an older man preparing for retirement with time on his hands, but a young man with a booming construction firm in our community. Tom stepped forward and volunteered to head the teams.

I don't think I will ever forget the determination in his eyes, when he said, "I live to do these kinds of missions trips. I'm not a missionary myself. I'm a contractor, but I would like to organize my company and schedule so that I could make two or three of these trips a year.

"Send me to the place where I can make the most impact."

We took Tom up on his offer and presented several options to him. He then gathered together people from various professions who were all willing and eager to make sacrifices to accomplish something significant in Papua, New Guinea. It was truly gratifying to be able to send these teams. The letter we received back from the missionaries was filled with praise for the quality and commitment that these teams had devoted to the tasks at hand.

I wish I could say that the moving of our church toward networking workers and releasing individuals into significant expressions in the missions field is something that we strategized from the outset. Embarrassing as it is to admit, however, the folks who have filled our congregational ranks were the ones who forced us to realize that the Holy Spirit is vitally at work in them.

I believe Tom, Sharon and her husband may well be models for future short-term missionaries. Tom's infectious dedication has been instilled in many people in our community. The approach to life manifested by these three is catching on. The stretch between our life-styles and values is being narrowed by their vision to reach out and change the world.

LAICIZING THE CHURCH

Thirty something people will be forcing the Church to face the fact that the Church works best as a lay movement. Due to the target audience our church attracts, we have set about deprofessionalizing our congregation. As vocational leaders in our congregation, we are moving more and more toward not doing the work ourselves; instead, we are recruiting, training and releasing others to do the work.

Why? Because I truly believe any position that is presently salaried can probably be done just as well—and perhaps even better—by several volunteers. If the Church at large is to be challenging enough to appeal to boomers and to harness our hearts, this practice will have to become common throughout churches and organizations in America.

Remember, we are *not* meant to be mere spectators; we are called to be active participators! And boomers subscribe wholeheartedly to this viewpoint. So those churches that will appeal to boomers for the long term are those that will cultivate and implement this kind of approach. Systems, messages and models such as Tom and Sharon, when presented to the boomer age-group, will challenge us to the long haul.

I know of two institutions—Regent College in Vancouver, Canada, is one of them—that presently offer a curriculum to equip and prepare lay persons for significant leadership roles. They're extremely successful and their graduates are having extraordinary impact in their respective churches. And others are doing the same. So much so, that *I am bold enough to predict at this time that the thirty something people will laicize the Church again.*

THE COMING BOOMER AGE WAVE

What will happen now that baby boomers are moving toward forty something? For starters, with boomers moving toward mid-life, more of our society naturally will take on a middle-aged look. And as baby boomers take to the leadership platform, the tone of our entire culture will begin to change.

The first change likely to happen is that society will become more and more conservative. For, as people tend to do when they age, we boomers will become far more conservative than we have been in the past. Cheryl Russell of American Demographics put it this way:

> The demographics are determining the trends. If you know the trends, you can see into the future.
>
> Why is it getting so hard to buy marijuana? Why has everyone turned against cocaine? Why is

everyone drinking Perrier or white wine instead of whiskey?

What's so bad about drinking and driving? Why are *Playboy* and *Penthouse* losing readers? Why isn't business booming for X-rated cable channels?

There is only one reason that these issues— drugs, drinking and pornography—have become major public concerns in past years. Americans are middle-aging.[6]

The first boomers celebrated their fortieth birthday in 1986. The last of us will reach this milestone in the year 2004. This spells the end of the free-wheeling teenage culture that has ruled Madison Avenue for the past decade.

Even TV beer commercials emphasize moderation, with such statements as "know when enough is enough." The conservative trends in our culture are being recognized by marketers.

One of the reasons for this trend is that we baby boomers are beginning to reassess our lives at midpoint. The sense of invincibility that filled our teens and early 20s has departed. We are now well aware of the limits of abuse that our bodies will take.

Mid-life concerns will now fill the minds of baby boomers in the next two to three decades. When I recently preached the message, titled "Facing the Fear of Insignificance," I was pleasantly startled to learn that this tape has been one of the top-sellers in our church's tape library, and is still a popular item.

The theme of this message deals with facing the fears and issues of mid-life crises. It also discusses taking a mid-life pulse and assessment of where we boomers are headed and how we're doing at this point in our lives. This message further discusses how to leap over the emotional hurdle of feeling as though we have wasted the first half of our lives, and culminates with the true definition of significance from a biblical standpoint.

One of the reasons that particular message has had such a powerful impact is that, in giving it, I quite accidentally struck a raw nerve in the minds and hearts of our congrega-

---

Many, of us baby boomers are in the process of reevaluating our current values and where we're going with our lives....And all who are inclined toward evangelism know that it is during these times when we are most open to the Lord.

---

tion. Because of this relevance, I plan to develop an entire series of messages on this subject to prepare all our congregation for mid-life crises and reevaluation.

Aging and Relevance

I can't imagine what our culture will be like with a third of America's population facing these issues and reevaluating their lives concurrently. It could be frightening. But, then again, it could challenge us in the Church to communicate better with the needs of this age-group, for the aging of boomers may prove to be one of the greatest open doors for the Church at this time.

Many, many of us baby boomers are in the process of reevaluating our current values and where we're going with our lives. The fear of living a life that has not achieved the dreams of youth is a gripping one. And all who are inclined toward evangelism know that it is during these transitional times in life when we are most open to the Lord.

Because boomers desperately want their lives to count for something, our mid-life crises over the next decade or so present the Church with one of its greatest opportunities to offer hope to our generation. We thirty somethings—now going on 40—deeply desire to be significant, and we are worried that it won't happen.

Can you in the Church help us to get plugged in? If so, we're ready to listen, willing and able to respond.

Aging and Spiritual Growth

I feel that, coinciding with the aging of baby boomers, more and more study will be given to faith and the stages of life. What you believe in your teens is quite different from the process of faith in mid-life or even in later life. An approach to spiritual growth that progresses all the way to death will become more and more important to people.

In catering to boomers for so long, our society and even the Church have tended to worship youth. But the worship of youth is now ending in our culture. We leaders may as well proclaim it officially dead and begin anew to develop a viable approach to our purpose in life. Then people will look forward to being octogenarians.

A perspective of spiritual growth that focuses on the end of one's life will come of age in the next couple of decades. I am personally conducting much research on this topic and conversing with experts about it. Although youth ministries have been a primary focus for a long time, I believe it will now become common to have a ministry emphasis dealing with aging.

Churches that have been targeting boomers should not be surprised to learn that, along with this preoccupation with aging, the topic of retirement centers is surfacing. Young boomer pastors find this subject a laughable topic. But I believe that retirement centers will be a very common topic of discussion in almost every local church across America.

Why? Boomer Christians may want to retire together. They will want to retire meaningfully, and it is very likely that the state of the economy will force them to retire in clusters.

Some planning time would be well invested in this direction. Perhaps we could get the jump on some of these trends and use them as a basis of ministry, even though we probably aren't ready to plunge in right now. So I don't advise a Sunday morning message just yet on aging meaningfully. But in the backs of our minds, we in the Church would do well to anticipate in what ways boomers will age differently than our parents did.

Aging and Neo-traditionalism

Along with our growing conservatism, as boomers age, we will also return to traditional values. Now, don't get too optimistic. We boomers will definitely age differently than did our folks.

Our return to traditional values will still carry with it the unique perspectives of the baby boomer's worldview. So I've termed this return to traditional values "neo-traditionalism," because it will be mixed with untraditional viewpoints. And these distinctives are what makes baby boomers unique.

Predicting the impact of aging, once again, Cheryl Russell has stated:

> The importance of the home, for example, is tempered by the baby boom's global perspective. The importance of marriage is tempered by this generation's unisex lifestyle. The importance of family is tempered by the rise of individualism, and the importance of work is tempered by the baby boomer's search for instant gratification.[7]

Even though boomers have been very poor at marriage relationships, we still have a high regard for marriage. The tendency toward excessive individualism has put a strain on boomer families. But, from a traditional standpoint, we value marriage highly.

Home life is another emphasis that will come upon boomers. Cocooning didn't quite catch on as was predicted. I suspect it is because, though we boomers like to talk about traditional home life, the way we carry it out is quite different.

The traditional evening meal around a table together has been replaced by Big Macs on the run. And even though boomers are moving toward greater health consciousness, and a bean sprout sandwich on stone-ground whole-wheat bread may replace a Big Mac, the fast pace of our culture will probably work against some memories boomers have of traditional home life. But home, nonetheless, remains a mighty important factor to boomers.

The boomers' penchant for instant gratification likewise affects our commitment to work. Employing baby boomers can in itself be an education in the fine points of instant gratification. Work is important to boomers and we will be loyal to your company, but we are most loyal to our own sense of accomplishment and to achieving goals on our own agendas.

So the search for new values may well have come to an end. Baby boomers are returning to old values, but in new ways. Any pastor whose message can guide boomers to a traditional life-style, but in boomer terms, will be very successful.

If, for instance, you're aware of the boomer's desire for a home life that is high on the individual, you will do well. If, as a pastor, you can present a series on "Why Work?" and yet emphasize what individuals can expect to take away from their jobs, boomers will listen eagerly to what you have to say. The secret of success is to be both neo-traditional and biblical at the same time.

Can you pull it off? It's worth trying!

PASTORAL CONCERNS FOR THE DECADE AHEAD

As I observe many thirty something folks coming into our church, I believe some stress points will need to be addressed in the not-too-distant future. I pastor a congregation on the West Coast of the United States, an area which tends to be a little more liberal in outlook than the rest of the nation, but I sense that—even though regional distinctions exist—we're really not all that different. So though I don't feel qualified to comment with authority beyond my own pastoral assignment, I feel the concerns I have for my congregation might still be of interest to others.

I have identified at least four areas that I'm carefully preparing to address our congregation on over the next several years. And I suspect these are concerns and issues that ought to be considered by our society and churches at large:

Universalism

When I share a message with our congregation, I usually start with the assumption that most of the people attending are greatly inclined toward universalism. Universalism is the belief that everyone will be saved. It teaches that a loving God would never judge anybody, that all persons throughout history—no matter how evil, even the devil himself—will find themselves in heaven.

American Christianity has always struggled with balancing the love of God with the justice of God, making the concept of a final judgment a difficult one to present to most congregations. But the confusing influence of Far Eastern philosophies have made the topics of judgment and accountability even more difficult to address when speaking to boomers. And the New Age belief in reincarnation has instilled a further belief in us that we have many opportunities to get our lives right.

But these unfounded, invalid influences run counter to the biblical teaching of one life and one call to accountability (see Heb. 9:27). So I must include in my messages and impress upon the minds of our thirty something congregation the unalterable fact that justice and accountability are biblical realities.

But, since a final judgment is a very unsavory topic to boomers, when I touch on it, I take time to explain it clearly yet delicately. For failure to mention judgment at all will not only weaken our spiritual fiber, but the moral fiber of our ranks as well.

As a pastor, my great challenge is to present God as being *for* people (see Ps. 8:4; Luke 13:34; John 3:16; 1 John 4:8-10,16,19), to show that God pronounced judgment upon mankind with reluctance (see Matt. 18:14; 2 Pet. 3:9) and to emphasize that the mission of God's Son was to make it possible for us to avoid this judgment (see John 3:15-18,36; Rom. 3:22-26; 1 John 4:14; 5:11-12).

How this is done will need to be uniquely tempered for the boomer society, but it is an issue that could greatly impact our churches in the days ahead. Meanwhile, we pastors have the challenge before us to convince our people, in a way that they will hear, that we are all accountable and face a final judgment. Great skill will be required to communicate these truths, but the effort must be put forth or our churches will run the risk of sounding more like Unitarian churches than the evangelical churches that they are.

Relativism and the Secular Mind-set

The second issue I see facing the people I lead is the extreme relativism of our society. We now live in the ultimate culture of pluralism. And we should celebrate the many strata and layers of culture that our society represents. But pluralism taken to extremes results in relativism. And *a relativism that releases us from the anchors of absolutes is deadly.*

There was a time when pastors could safely assume that the majority of people in their congregations were thinking from a biblical frame of reference. Today, when I stand to speak, however, I am aware that the majority of those attending our church have a predominantly secular mind-set.

And just as universalism-oriented people have difficulty believing that God would judge anyone, those with a secular mind-set have as much difficulty accepting the concept of eternal absolutes, such as believing the authoritative statements of Scripture to be God's final declaration. We may give verbal assent to this truth, but the mental force of our culture so works against such an absolute belief that, as a pastor, I must restate over and over why I believe in the authoritative statements of Scripture.

Hopefully, if I do a good job, week by week, and the various training mechanisms in our congregation take hold, we can allow ourselves to be evangelistically sensitive, yet have a congregation that is entrenched in a biblical frame of reference.

The Desire for Instant Gratification

Our generation's insistence on instant gratification is an issue that concerns me greatly. As a pastor, I've seen the damage that instant gratification can cause in a person's life. And as someone who desires to evangelize the thirty something group, I'm aware that this tendency could be one of the greatest obstacles for us in the Church to overcome.

Though a life-style of instant gratification does lend itself to quick decisions, many resulting decisions for Christ are often shortsighted and incomplete. This penchant for instant gratification, therefore, will be a great deterrent to discipling this generation, for such a life-style does not commend itself to the call of lifelong discipleship.

A related issue is that our desire for instant gratification causes us boomers to want immediate gratification from our worship experience. Not only will we baby boomers not search for a church for months on end, we fully expect to go once to a church and be gratified by our first experience there. And if our expectations of a worship setting aren't met the first or maybe a second time, it may be many years before we will even try again.

The idea of investing time, effort and resources in a local fellowship so as to receive the kind of life desired is quite foreign to baby boomers. Church leaders who seek to attract boomers must understand this particular perspective of our generation and recognize that dealing with it will place an extreme amount of pressure upon them. But the persevering pastor who is in there for the long haul will unquestionably reap results in changed lives and an enlarged ministry to the thirty something crowd.

Doctrinal Instruction Balances Spiritual Experiences

I get really excited about the reality of spiritual experiences. Yet, I sense that we could easily lose our underpinnings in the coming decade if we church leaders do not make a conscious effort to introduce biblical content and doctrine creatively and systematically to our people.

We will undoubtedly find it necessary to create effective ways and formulas for presenting solid biblical teaching and the formulation of clear doctrine to boomer believers. Initially, this element will not attract boomers, as it would their elders, to our congregation. But it will be necessary to the spiritual health of the church, and—perhaps at first to some—as nutritionally necessary and unappealing as eating broccoli.

The challenge is ever before us as leaders to keep this tension between instruction and experience a healthy one, if we are to lead this generation into the future with a vigorous spiritual foundation. We have faced this issue in our own congregation by developing a department we have designated as the Institute of Applied Ministries. We are also devising an entire strategy that sometimes uses other felt needs in attracting people to gatherings where doctrine and biblical content can be taught.

For example, in our Institute of Applied Ministries, we have incorporated serious courses on theology, church growth and biblical studies that are required for those who wish to take significant roles of leadership in our church. A number of these courses have even received accreditation through qualified leaders affiliated with a college here in the Northwest. It's been rewarding to see some of our leaders grow in Bible knowledge and understanding. They have returned to me afterwards with such statements as "now I know why we do what we do."

Another example of instilling biblical content into the lives of our people is through women's Bible studies. Because we understand that everyone has a high need for fellowship, the initial attraction of these studies is the opportunity to get together, to share one another's needs and to pray for one another. But primarily, we use these gatherings as opportunities to infuse the women with intense Bible study.

As mentioned before, we have the course entitled "Church 101." This course embodies our church's philosophy and values, as well as the doctrine of ecclesiology. As individuals work through this course, they will become fairly well indoctrinated with Jesus' concept of the Kingdom of God and the Church of Jesus Christ.

In addition, we've worked long and hard to make certain that our home study groups remain thoroughly biblical, even while we also meet many practical needs in both our community and our church. Each home group studies Romans and Ephesians to bring Scripture content into their lives.

We have added a theologian-in-residence to our staff. The reason we took this action was because I felt the strong need for spiritual experiences in our culture could draw us away from sound theological underpinnings. Not being a theologian myself, I believed it was necessary to have someone who could look at just about everything we do from a theological perspective. Taking this action has been one of the wisest steps we've ever taken and one that I feel will ensure the spiritual health of our congregation in the decades ahead.

WHO WILL BE FIRST AND HOW?

Cheryl Russell, in her book, *100 Predictions for the Baby Boomer: The Next 50 Years*, challenges political parties at the national level to learn from the great "New Coke mistake" of the 1980s.[7]

You probably remember the announcement by Coca-Cola that they were going to cease producing Coke as we have known it. Traditionally, soft drinks have been consumed by people in their 20s and 30s. The bigwigs at Coca-Cola, believing younger people like sweeter products, had decided their product wasn't as sweet as their competitor's. So Coca-Cola determined that they would make a sweeter Coke.

The announcement that a newer, sweeter Coke would replace the Coke we had always enjoyed resulted in an immediate national uproar. It was caused by boomers, for the most part, who wanted to continue enjoying their traditional Coke. As far as boomers were concerned, the CEOs (chief executive officers) at Coca-Cola were trying to remove one of the great trademarks of our culture, and the thirty something folks refused to let that happen.

You may recall the embarrassing announcement that appeared a few weeks later: Coca-Cola would continue to produce traditional Coke under the name of "Classic Coke." And "New Coke," with more sweetening and the same amount of caffeine as the traditional Coke, would also be produced. The amazing fact is that today Classic Coke remains overwhelmingly more popular than New Coke.

Russell suggests that this Classic Coke/New Coke debacle teach a lesson to us all. Large conglomerates and political parties would do well to realize the power this boomer generation possesses. I would add that this same event could be a lesson to churches and church leaders as well to learn. Though Coca-Cola is hardly as important an issue as those we face in the Church, their hard-learned lesson is worth our attention: *Ignore this generation and its appeals, and you will pay the price.*

The question is not whether this generation will be challenged to rise to its destiny or that their newfound concern for changes in the world will be tapped by middle-aged boomers. The big question is: Who will be the first to catch the boomer's ear?

The competition is strong, for quasi-religions and human potential movements are already catching their ears. New religions, including the New Age movement and cults, will all attempt to appeal to the boomer perspective. I have horrific thoughts that some ill-motivated political party—perhaps even one of a Nazi type—will suddenly realize the void in boomer leadership and step into that void.

The interest that the Church is beginning to express in boomers is moving beyond a faddish concern—and that excites me. The Church may just be the one to get there first. And apparently, at this time, thirty something people are willing to give us a chance. Are we ready for them?

Someone will reach the baby boomers and, as Paula Rinehart stated in her article, "The Pivotal Generation," which appeared in *Christianity Today*: "The question is not so much if this generation's latent idealism can be tapped, but who will be first and how?"[8]

The Church will be a step ahead if we seize this opportunity. And with good planning and open-hearted forethought, I know we can be there first!

Notes
1. Landon Jones, *Great Expectations: America and the Baby Boom Generation* (New York: Ballantine Books, 1986), p. 387.
2. Cheryl Russell, *What's Going to Happen When the Baby Boom Gets*

Older? (Ithaca, NY: American Demographics, 1987), p. 2.
3. Paula Rinehart, "The Pivotal Generation," *Christianity Today,* October 6, 1989, p. 26.
4. Cheryl Russell, *100 Predictions for the Baby Boom: The Next 50 Years* (New York: Plenum Press, 1987), p. 160.
5. Ibid.
6. Cheryl Russell, *What's Going to Happen,* p. 2.
7. Ibid., p. 4.
8. Cheryl Russell, *100 Predictions for the Baby Boom,* pp. 48-49.
9. Paula Rinehart, "The Pivotal Generation," p. 26.

BIBLIOGRAPHY

BOOKS

Carnes, Patrick, Ph.D. *Out of the Shadows: Understanding Sexual Addiction.* Minneapolis: CompCare Publishers, 1983.

Cook, Barbara. *Ordinary Women, Extraordinary Strength: A Biblical Perspective of Feminine Potential.* Lynnwood, WA: Aglow Publications, 1988.

Evans, Mary J. *Women in the Bible.* Downers Grove, IL: InterVarsity Press, 1984.

Foh, Susan T. *Women and the Word of God.* Phillipsburg, NJ: Presbyterian & Reformed Publishing Co., 1979.

Gilligan, Carol. *In a Different Voice.* Cambridge: Harvard University Press, 1982.

Gundry, Patricia. *Neither Slave, Nor Free: Helping Women Answer the Call to Church Leadership.* New York: Harper & Row, 1987.

Jones, Landon. *Great Expectations: America and the Baby Boom Generation.* New York: Ballantine Books, 1986.

Kritsberg, Wayne. *The Adult Children of Alcoholics.* Pomona Beach, FL: Health Communications, Inc., 1985.

Larsen, Earnie. *Stage Two Recovery: Life Beyond Addiction.* New York: Harper & Row, 1985.

Light, Paul C. *The Baby Boomers.* New York: W.W. Norton & Co., 1988.

Lyon, William. *A Pew for One, Please: the Church and the Single Person.* New York: Crossroads Books, Seabury Press, [n.d.].

Martin, Faith. *Call Me Blessed: The Emerging Christian Woman.* Grand Rapids, MI: Eerdman's Publishing Co., 1988.

Martin, Sara Hines. *Healing for Adult Children of Alcoholics.* Nashville: Broadman Press, 1988.

Myers, David G. *Social Psychology.* New York: McGraw-Hill Book Co., 1983.

Neff, David. *Tough Questions Christians Ask.* Wheaton, IL: Victor Books, 1989.

Peter, Laurence J. *Peter's Quotations: Ideas for Our Time.* New York: Bantam Books, 1979.

Russell, Cheryl. *What's Going to Happen When the Baby Boom Gets Older?* Ithaca, NY: American Demographics, 1987.

Russell, Cheryl. *One Hundred Predictions for the Baby Boom: The Next Fifty Years.* New York: Plenum Press, 1987.

Sayers, Dorothy L. *Are Women Human?* Grand Rapids, MI: Eerdman's Publishing Co., 1971.

Schaller, Lyle. *It's a Different World.* Nashville: Abingdon Press, 1987.

Schussler-Fiorenza, Elizabeth. *A Feminist Theological Reconstruction of Christian Origins.* New York: Crossroads Press, 1984.

Simon, Sidney B., ed. *Getting Unstuck.* New York: Warner Books, 1989.

Storkey, Elaine. *What's Right with Feminism?* Grand Rapids: Eerdman's Publishing Co., 1986.

Wegscheider-Cruse, Sharon. *The Miracle of Recovery: Healing for Addicts, Adult Children and Co-Dependents.* Deerfield Beach, FL: Health Communications, Inc., 1989.

Woititz, Janet Garringer. *Adult Children of Alcoholics.* Deerfield Beach, FL: Health Communications, Inc., 1983.

Woititz, Janet Garringer. *Struggle for Intimacy.* Deerfield Beach, FL: Health Communications, Inc., 1985

JOURNALS, NEWSPAPERS, PERIODICALS

Associated Press dispatch. *Tacoma* [WA] *News Tribune*, March 29, 1990.

"Average U.S. Citizen: Married Woman, 32." *USA Today*, May 15, 1989.

Boomer Report 1, no. 1 (April 1989). New York: Find/SVP, Inc.

Boomer Report 1, no. 12 (March 1990). New York: Find/SVP, Inc.

Gallup, George. *Emerging Trends* 1, no. 8 (1988). Princeton: Princeton Religion Research Center.

Gallup, George. *Emerging Trends* 2, no. 3 (1989). Princeton: Princeton Religion Research Center.

Hayden, Tom. "Decade Shock." *Newsweek*, September 5, 1988: 14.

"Monday." *USA Today*, May 15, 1989: A-3.

"Nationline." *USA Today*, January 1, 1988.

Rinehart, Paula. "The Pivotal Generation." *Christianity Today*, October 6, 1989: 26.

"Will We Ever Get Over the Sixties?" *Newsweek*, September 5, 1988.

LECTURE

Simms, Jack. "Why Are These People Smiling? Because They Don't Have to Go to Church Anymore." Pasadena, CA: Fuller Theological Seminary [n.d.].

REPORTS

Barna, George. "Seven Trends Facing the Church in 1988 and Beyond." *National and International Religion Report*.

Barna, George. "Single Adults in America." Glendale, CA: Barna Research Group, 1987.

"The Unchurched American Ten Years Later." Princeton: Princeton Religion Research Center, 1988.

DEMCO